Diaries of an Isle Royale Fisherman

Diaries of an Isle Royale Fisherman

Elling Seglem

Robert Root and Jill Burkland
Editors

Isle Royale Natural History Association
Houghton, Michigan

Copyright 2002 by the Isle Royale Natural History Association
Houghton, Michigan

ISBN 0-935289-13-5

Library of Congress Control Number: 2002112588

Project Management by Jill Burkland

Book Design and Layout by Mike Stockwell, Cranking Graphics

Printed by The Book Concern, Hancock, Michigan

Photos Supplied by the Isle Royale National Park Collection and Gloria Covert

Passage Island
Lighthouse

Belle Isle

Todd
Harbor

Tobin Harbor

Rock Harbor

Siskiwit
Lake

Isle Royale Lighthouse (Menagerie Island)

Seglem's Isle Royale

9

Introduction

When I read my first issue of the Fisherman's Home Journal, dated June 21, 1920, "Issued 'Weakly' for those who like to read FISH STORIES," I immediately realized that Elling Seglem was someone I wanted to know better. I had learned his name and became curious about him a number of years earlier when I ran across some photos in the archives with "E.A. Seglem" and "4514 North Troy Street, Chicago, Illinois," on the back. They were in the Fred Dustin collection, so I always assumed that he was either a photographer who accompanied Dustin on his 1929-1930 archeological survey or one of the fishermen Dustin ran across on the island. I didn't know that he was both photographer and fisherman. Then, in 1997, Seglem's great granddaughter from California sent a message asking for information about the island, and specifically Seglem's Harbor, or Fisherman's Home Cove as it was also called, because her great grandfather, Elling Seglem, spent the summers from 1917 to 1932 fishing there. Fisherman's Home is a sheltered harbor on the south shore of Isle Royale just outside Siskiwit Bay. She also mentioned that her mother had diaries, photos, and letters from Elling and wondered if Isle Royale National Park or the Natural History Association were interested in them. Of course, we were immediately interested, so she sent us copies.

With these materials in the Isle Royale archives, we were able to get closer to knowing who Elling Seglem was. From his family, and from the diaries and letters, we have been able to find out that Elling Seglem came to this country from Seglem, Norway, in 1879 with his mother and sister. He was 15 when he made the journey and adopted Seglem as his last name when he arrived. The family originally joined relatives in Iowa before settling in Chicago, where jobs were plentiful. Mr. Seglem was a professional photographer. He started visiting Fisherman's Home Cove on Isle Royale in 1917 and spent most summers there until his last in 1932. How did this Norwegian-born professional photographer come to spend his summers at Isle Royale? Elling was not alone in his venture. He joined his cousin, Edward T. Seglem, (or E.T., as he is referred to in the diaries), a commercial fisherman. E.T. was on the island by 1900 and possibly earlier. E.T., along with his wife, Alida, and son Thorwald are listed in the 1900 census for Isle Royale. Often, Elling's wife, Almida, and some or all of his five children, Clarence, Edith, Alice, Esther, and Roy, accompanied him to Fisherman's Home.

Elling's writings reflect a joy at being at Isle Royale, a wonderful command of English, and abundant good natured humor about life on the island, including some of the less desirable aspects such as the endless flapjacks (pancakes) for breakfast and fish for many meals, the "lovely mosquitoes and black flies," that sometimes made his face and neck swell up, and the weather, that occasionally kept him from getting out in the boat. He tells of the early mornings getting up at 4 or 5 to start fishing and of getting forced off the lake by fog or rowing home in a heavy sea. His writings give a good view of life at a working fishery during this time, although Elling was not a commercial fisherman by trade. Most serious commercial fishermen in the period, like his cousin and most of his neighbors, set either gill nets or hook lines from wooden gas boats. They caught hundreds of pounds of fish which they shipped to market in Duluth on the *America* or other steamer. Elling, on the other hand, usually caught his fish by rowing in a small boat and trolling with a hook and line. He occasionally set a net. One summer he tried a net borrowed from Hans Mindstrom, another fisherman who lived in Little Boat Harbor, the next cove down the shoreline. And he didn't always row his boat. According to his list of expenditures in 1921, he paid $60 for an engine, but often ended up rowing anyway because it was not always in working order. Elling spent hours rowing his boat for miles, and often commented how worn out he was from it at the end of the day.

Elling individually counted the fish that he sent on the steamer and was paid for them by the pound. In the records he kept for 1923, his largest shipment was 88 lbs for which he received $9.68 or 11 cents per pound. The income he received no doubt supplemented his regular job, and provided cash for the summers on the island, but wouldn't have provided enough to live on. When the steamer came by every couple of days, the residents of the narrow harbor had to go out to meet it with their smaller boat and pass fish, mail and often passengers and gear back and forth while floating on the water. Large steamers, like the *America* and the *Easton,* couldn't make it into many of the shallow harbors along the route around the island.

A trip to Isle Royale from Chicago in the 1920s was vastly different than today. Seglem traveled by train from Chicago across Wisconsin to Duluth, stopping overnight a few times in Viroqua, a small town that is the county seat of Vernon County, Wisconsin. The trip took him to Duluth, where he boarded the steamer *America* and traveled first up the north shore of Minnesota, stopping at many of the small communities such as Two Harbors, Beaver Bay, Cross River, and Tofte, to Grand Marais and Grand Portage, before heading out to Isle Royale. The trip took Seglem about a week, depending on how long he visited in Duluth before heading out. The *America* made the run from Duluth up the north shore to Fort William and Port Arthur, circumnavigating Isle Royale two to three times a week, providing regular passenger and freight service to the island from 1902 until it hit a reef in the fog and sank on the west end of the island in June 1928.

Many people traveling on the steamers at this time were vacationing tourists. Visitors had a choice of resorts once they got to Isle Royale. On the north shore, Belle Isle Resort offered a small golf course and rustic cabins. On the east end of the island, visitors could stay at Minong Lodge in Tobin Harbor, Rock Harbor Lodge, or Tourist Home on what is now Davidson Island. Washington Island boasted the Singer resort, with a dance hall and bowling alley. A large community of summer residents with cabins around Isle Royale also utilized the steamers to get to Isle Royale. Concentrated in Tobin and Rock Harbors, on Barnum Island, and on the north shore near Belle Isle, more than 50 families spent part of their summers on the island.

Seglem's writings give a wonderful sense of the fishing community in the 1920s and 1930s. On his way to the island, Seglem would stop and visit the Skadbergs, fishermen from Hay Bay. While on the island, he often got together with his neighbors, Martin Halloran, who lived on Halloran Lake, and Hans Mindstrom, from Little Boat Harbor. The fishing community included the hired men working for fishermen, as well as families and bachelors. Another family of fishermen, the Rudes, joined the Seglems at Fishermen's Home some time in the 1920s. A third generation Rude still lives at Fishermen's Home during the summer, using and maintaining some of the buildings that the Seglems built. Elling often visited the Hay Bay fishermen, the Skadbergs and Andersons, and occasionally other fishermen from around the island stopped by to visit him. One year on his way in from the island he traveled to Washington Harbor and spent a few days visiting the fishermen at Washington and Booth Islands. The 4th of July was the social event of the summer for the fishermen. In the 1932 diary, Elling goes into detail about a trip to Chippewa Harbor for a celebration with music and dancing.

The final diary from 1932 was Elling's last year on the island. His son, Roy, and new daughter-in-law, Eleanora, accompanied him to Isle Royale on their honeymoon. In this diary, he frequently writes of the stomach trouble he was experiencing at the time, "felt peculiar as my stomach was not working right." This is evidently part of the problem that lead to Seglem's death of colon cancer in 1934.

We are so fortunate that the Seglem family was willing to make Elling's diaries available for us. They give a glimpse of a way of life spanning two decades that doesn't exist anymore, on Isle Royale or anywhere. It is part of a larger story; it is America's history, not just Isle Royale's. Elling and his family and fishermen friends will live on in our memories thanks to his efforts at documenting his life and thanks to his family's willingness to preserve and share what he left behind.

Liz Valencia
Branch Chief for Cultural Resources
Isle Royale National Park

A note on the text

The original texts of the writing by Elling A. Seglem consulted for this book are in the possession of family members. Not all the original manuscripts still exist; in some cases all that survives is a typed manuscript, leaving the editors to trust the accuracy of the typist's reading of the manuscript rather than allowing them to read (or misread) the manuscript themselves. In some cases the editors have been assisted by members of a graduate text editing class at Central Michigan University, and family members have been consulted about dubious or problematic interpretations and identification of individuals mentioned in the texts.

Two documents among this writing were originally written by Elling Seglem to imitate the format and tone of newspapers. Seglem was a photographer and had experience with publishing and used doctored cartoons and illustrations out of newspapers to serve as illustrations for his Fisherman's Home Journal (1920) and The Fish Scale (1932). In 1932 his Fish Scale was a response to a weekly newsletter from home, edited and compiled by his son and daughter, Clarence and Edith, titled The Weekly Hoozis. The same year his son and daughter-in-law, Roy and Eleanora, who were honeymooning at the fish camp, compiled a similar newsletter, The Fish News. Except for a poem from 1919, "The Call of the Wild," which exists only in typescript, the diaries from 1921, 1923, 1924, and 1932 were kept in standard diary format. The 1932 diary covers the same period as The Fish Scale and gives us an opportunity to see the difference between Elling's private diary and the public document produced for his family.

Elling's spelling is idiosyncratic, partly because of the circumstances of his composing and partly because of his tendency to make jokes and imitate dialect in writing. For example, he almost always refers to pancakes as "flop jacks" rather than "flapjacks," and often refers to a bird as a "boid." Often the editors have been uncertain whether a misspelling was a mistake or a deliberate attempt at wordplay. In addition, his punctuation is uneven because he was often writing on the fly and adding new sections to sentences after he had already completed them. Finally, he tosses in a number of Norwegian words and phrases, some of which are spelled more phonetically than regularly. All of these factors have produced challenges to the accuracy and uniformity of our transcription.

We have, therefore, elected to produce a more readable version of Elling's manuscript by silently emending some spelling, capitalization, and punctuation throughout these texts. We have attempted to provide accurate spellings of place names and personal names. For example, Siskiwit, as an Isle Royale regular knows, can be spelled several different ways depending on whether it refers to a fish, a mining location, a bay, lake, or river; we have opted to use the spelling to be found on the map when referring to Siskiwit Bay, in order to reduce reader confusion. Similarly, Elling's daughter-in-law, Eleanora, a character in the 1932 material, has her name spelled three different ways in the original manuscript, none of which was the correct spelling (which may be the reason he eventually referred to her as either "El" or "L"). Regularizing some features of spelling and punctuation has not meant that we have "corrected" the texts thoroughly, since that would eliminate much of the charm, wit, and idiosyncrasy of Elling's writing.

The illustrations that appear in The Fisherman's Home Journal and The Fish Scale are more problematic, since very often they provide a reference point for Elling's remarks in writing. They were clipped from newspapers, very likely old editions of the Chicago Tribune or other papers being mailed to the island, and often emended to serve Elling's particular joke. One example is the accompanying panel, which appeared in "Harold Teen," a popular comic strip which appeared in the July 4, 1920 edition of the *Chicago Sunday Tribune*. With an inked-on moustache to change the look of the character and a label on the bowl to identify the product, the original panel serves as a visual component of the comment in the newsletter. Elling sometimes traced and modified original images but most often he simply clipped and adapted the material.

Original panel

Elling's adaptation

We have endeavored without much success to locate the original panels for the comic strips, advertising illustrations, and editorial cartoons Elling used. While some seem to have been from the period in which they were used, others may have been from newspapers, magazines, or catalogues which have not been preserved in historical archives or libraries. Since Elling simply glued images to the page and wrote by hand around them, he had less difficulty with text wrapping than the book's designer who has attempted to preserve Elling's style. We have modified the relationship between image and text where necessary, reproducing the most relevant and crucial images, but inserting typeset text to enhance legibility.

Robert Root

"The Call of the Wild"

O come with me to Northern Clime,
    Away from town and strife
Come next to Nature, most sublime,
    Enjoy the "only" life.

Way out in Lake Superior
    We have a land so fair,
Where freedom reigns upon its shore
    And drives away your cares.

Where nature wild in jungle lurks
    And fragrant blossoms grow,
There stands my cabin 'mongst the birch
    While balmy zephyrs blow.

Amongst the fir and mountain ash
    And balsam and the birch,
For cedar and the scented air
    We do not have to search.

Isle Royale, fair, beyond compare,
    A rest for weary soul
Is found right there in clime so rare
    Wherever we may stroll.

Thy waters blue and crystal clear,
    Your flowing cup we drain
We love your bays and shores so dear
    In sunshine and in rain.

Your garden wild, O fairest child!
    The tiny beauties grow
With scent so pure— a heaven sure,
    From spring till early snow.

The little blue lobelias
    And bluebells by the score
With phlox and shiny buttercups
    They line the rocky shore.

The cherry blossoms and the rose
    In merry riot stand,
Their perfume sweet in waves they meet
    And bid you shake their hand.

And up the cliff with roots so stiff
    The cedar clutches strong;
Up in the trees in gentle breeze
    We hear the warbler's song.

The Gull, O bird, you're always heard
    Lamenting forth your woe;
High in the tree-tops flits and flops
    The blackest mournful crow.

Each morning gay, when in the bay
    We hear the laughing loon,
While rowing out our line for trout
    With shining hooks and spoon.

The fish beguiled, in little while
    Is tugging on the line;
A little trial—a broadened smile—
    O trout, I call you mine!

A meal of fish— a dainty dish,
    For beef I wouldn't trade;
Our appetite is "out-o-site"
    When sumptuous dinner's made.

Isle Royale's shore, forever more
    In mem'ry will endure,
When far from here in Southern sphere
    We hail thy wondrous lure!

                    Elling Andreas Seglem.

Fisherman's Home, Isle Royale.
    August 9, 1919.

17

Fisherman's Home Journal.

ISSUED "WEAKLY" for those who like to read FISH STORIES

No. 1. ISLE ROYAL, MICH. Week Ending June 21, 1920

Monday June 14th

Got up early and as it was a fine Morning, I hurried up with breakfast and went out in the bay for a tryout. The skiff is fairly dry after being newly painted. Pretty light too. Shoved her into water myself and she leaks very little after being on land for 10 months. She looks spick and span with her new coat of lead gray paint. Some craft I'll say.

Poor luck today—only one poor feesh. Wind started to blow up. Hiked home. Cleaned my fish for the Steamer.* Had 9 trout shipped, fairly good start. Better than I expected.

Oh man, I got pretty well sunburned while out in the bay—Sun boiling hot. Think my neck will blister. It's pretty sore. My nose looks beautiful.

Had a beautiful supper—one that will make anybody's mouth water. A nice juicy 1 1/2 lb. Brook trout fried to perfection, and hot spuds, Coffee, fresh bread, butter, cheese, and a big dish of my famous rice for a side dish. Had to loosen up my pants to make room for all of it.

Received word that Alice* had left for Duluth. Hope she has a nice trip.

Sent letter to home and felt happy. Went to bed with the sun and Slept well.

Tuesday, June 15th

Woke up at 6 G.M.* A gale blowing. Looked out—no weather for fishing. Went back to bed again and slept till 8. Got up and made breakfast. Eat 4 big slices of bread and drank 3 cups of coffee. Cooked another pot of rice and stowed away a big dish.

Bailed out the boat and christened her "ALICE S." Alice will be tickled when she sees her name on the boat.

Alice and the Alice S.

Hope weather moderates so I can get out and hook up a few for Thursday's steamer.

Had dinner at Edward's.* He is busy painting up his big boat.

Bad day on the lake. Blowing all day. Wind died out towards sunset. Couldn't get out at all.

Painted Edward's boat a bright white. Put oarlocks on "ALICE S."

Am now preparing my lonesome supper. Fried Brooktrout and other good things. Wish Ma* was here to get some of this good fish.

You tell 'em fish—you're in the swim. This is the real life.

It looks as if I'm getting fat—but anyhow my whiskers are growing nicely—and my face is resuming its usual fishy color. —red.

The feed is now stowed away—O Man! The Kink of Denmark couldn't feel better than I do just now. Well good dite.

Wednesday June 16th

Well, good morning, folks! Yes, thank you, I slept fairly well, but once in a while I woke up from the noise of a furious gale blowing through the trees and the seawater roaring against the rocky shore. Sweet music I'll say.

Made a 10 story stack of Aunt Jemima's. Well, it would do your heart good to see me pack 'em away. With juicy syrup and hot java I tell you they slid down mighty well. Smack, Smack, Smack.

Went over to the beach and picked a swell bouquet of wild flowers for my table. Well, it really looks like a florist's shop in the shack. O Nature thou art glorious!

Wind still blowing strong and big sea running. Hope it will moderate. Alice leaves Duluth this A.M. for here. Hope she won't get sea sick.

Too bad. The weather will not permit me to go out on the lake so I can get a few for tomorrow's Steamer. O heart o' mine, why should you worry so?

What do you know about it? I saw wood!

That fountain pen I got from Ed comes in mighty handy—but how do you like the color of this ink? Some shade!

Out on the lake all afternoon. In Siskiwit* Bay and way out around Redfin Island.* Caught one lonely 5 pounder. Yes, Ma'm, the weather is getting very nice in afternoon.

Guess I'll shave. I look like JoJo the dogfaced man. Some crop I'll say.

Thursday June 17th

"Well, how do you do, folks, here I am right off the boat. I certainly had a most delightful trip and just think—I didn't get seasick. And the splendid eats we had on the boat an' ev'rything!"

"What a lovely place you have here, folks. Oh, my, I'm so glad I came. And oh there is a boat with my name on it, an' ev'rything.
And what lovely flowers you have on the table and the delightful smell of fish, an' ev'rything!

And right away we have a birth-day Party (Magda's*) and what a lovely birthday cake Mrs. Seglem* has made with candles on it, an' ev'rything!

And the lovely mosquitoes and black flies and nice gulls, and big trees, an' every thing!

And now, I'm going to have a lovely boat ride in Pa's lovely boat that he's named after me an' ev'rything.

Oh, if the folks at home only knew how happy I am they would surely be tickled to a stand still.
JERUSHA*

21

Friday June 18th

Went out trolling in Siskiwit Bay. Caught 6 good sized Trout. One a 17 pounder.

While out in the bay, I noticed a little boat, painted a grass green color, and with a figure clad in a khaki shirt, coming my way. First I took it for the Game Warden. But on closer examination I found it to be the hero of my story, Martin Halloran.* He was heading for Fisherman's Home.

"Be dad," says he to me, " I want you to go along with me to my cabin when I go home this afternoon." And as I was very much interested in his place in the jungle, I gladly accepted his invitation.

Started out for his place at 2 p.m. and reached it at 6 p.m. Some row (6 miles). Some hike through the forest (1 mile). Some ride on his raft (1 mile) up the little inland lake.

Slept with my hero and he is some storyteller. A quaint old character. A gentleman.

Took several Pictures of the place. Saw 3 big moose and got one of the antlers as a souvenir of the place.

Halloran's Cabin

Saturday June 19th

Woke up alongside of my friend Halloran about 4 A.M. He was also awake and started talking politics and other subjects until both of us fell asleep again and didn't wake up till 6 A.M.

Old Halloran throws a few logs into his oldfashion fireplace and makes breakfast—Skoan bred* (Made while you wait) Coffee, rice pudding, bacon and beans. I tell you it tastes mighty fine when you are 700 miles from nowhere and a "holy appetite" gnawing your insides.

Martin Halloran

After breakfast we took a stroll into the dense jungle for about a mile or so. Some jungle, I'll say. Full of mosquitoes.

After that 9:30 A.M. I started back for home 9 miles away. Halloran poled me down the little lake on his great raft for a mile, to the east end of the lake (his cabin is at the west end) and followed me halfway across the trail in the forest so I wouldn't get lost. I trudged through the rest of the way to where my boat was, all alone. That's some hike, I'll say, through the dense timber where the sun never shines. Reached the shore at 11 o'clock and after a row of 7 miles reached home at 1:30 p.m.

On the way coming and going I picked up several big trout.

I might tell you I was pretty "holy" inside when I got back from the trip and Alice prepared a big dinner (she's some cook, I'll say). She and I went trolling. We picked up 3 trout—one a 17 pounder, but the wind was strong and the lake choppy so we couldn't pursue our pleasure with greater success.

23

Sunday June 20th

Good morning, folks (rubber stamp). Feel pretty good. Had a fair night's sleep. Let's see. Oh yes, I think I'll make some of my famous flap jacks this morning. Ah, smack, smack, smack! They are good.

They must be good, for Alice says they are and she ought to know.

We're invited over to Edward's for dinner. Am so full of flapjacks—I don't think I can eat dinner.

I'm going out on the lake this P.M. and see if I can get a 30 pounder so as to break my last year's record. It's a fine day—so it is.

Some appetite Alice has made mash on up here—you ought to see her put the grub to the bad. Oh Henry!

Well, oh yes, I feel 2% better now. Had fish pudding for washdown.

Just back from the bay. Not much luck. Caught 2 poor feesh. One a 10-pounder.

Well, I'll have some fish for tomorrow's boat any how. So I should worry, but I won't.

My arms and face is like tan bark and Alice has acquired a beautiful, brilliant red nose.

She seems to like it out here. Of course I can't blame her. She went out fishing with me yesterday and got some fine mosquito bites on her neck.

På samma gongen får jog helsa hem til alla, I från basemeutet til taget. Go-na-at.*

Lively There

Our Game Warden's name is <u>Wm</u> Lively, and he promises to apply his name to any-
one who oversteps the game laws of this region whether on land or water. He has
been here all winter trapping. Caught 11 Wolves* and a large number of minks
and other wild animals. Occupied Edward's shack for a while and caught several
wolves right around the house. He also poisoned one but it got away from him
and he didn't find it again. Hans* and I found its tail and some of its fur scattered
over on the beach among the trees. Other wolves had evidently devoured it after
it had died from Lively's poison. I have the tail as a souvenir and will take it home
with me.

Started my keg of fish with a lonely 5-pounder—Well so long.

Elling with moose antler and "wolf" tail

Monday June 21

Aw, what's the use? It's blowing too hard. I won't get out o' bed yet—and it's only 5 o'clock. No lake weather. I'll snooze in again and take the world easy.

What! Half past eight? For the love of Fish, have I slept that long? Such a lazy bum!

Good morning, Alice, did you really wake up? Up so early (11^{00} A.M.) and not crying? This is really too early to get up—better go back to bed.

Well, today is steamboat day and we'll get lots of letters and newspapers from home.

The sea is running high and the wind is still blowing, but I've got to get out and get my fish that is sunk in the lake, and clean it for the Steamer.

Alice and the girls* are going out to the boat. They feel gay.

You tell 'em, Capt,* we got you on the run. Well, old Indian, Thank you very much for the candy you handed the girls. You're some gay sea dog, I'll say.

Poor Alice, she got no mail.

Tuesday, June 22

Same luck—raining and blowing. So what's the use? Can't go on the lake this morning either. Too bad—but "what I can do?"

Had a funny dream. Thought I was taking part in a Maccabee initiation* and woke up in the middle of the night shouting—"Fortunately indeed are we to have escaped from those cruel barbarians!"

Made a pot of my beautiful rice again and cooked prunes also. And of course we had flapjacks for breakfast.

Alice did fairly well today—she got up at 9^{30}.

Wind died down to a dead calm at noon and the lake got smooth. Alice and I rowed to the Rocks* trolling but with no success; then to McCormick's reefs with same results. Started from home at 12^{00}, got to the reefs at 2^{00}, and home again at 6^{00}. Some row I'll say—about 20 miles.

Alice is getting pretty well burned up and her appetite is improved nicely.

Alice at the Fish House

That's Telling—

Red as a lobster, fine as a fish;
In the wilderness bosom
I'm dwelling;
But one thing is lacking! This is my wish;
That Almida* was here with
her Elling

Wednesday, June 23

"Oh, ain't they cute? Look at them going, O, O, O. Well, what are they anyway—O, look at them going!"

They are a bunch or hatch of baby hell divers,* Alice; and there is the old Mother Duck with them. She's only got about 8 or 9. There are usually 14 or more in the hatch. The old duck must have been snitching on the job.

"Come back here, old man, you can't get away like that if I know it." Alice hooked onto a 12-pounder and bravely hauled it right close up to the boat and just as she was going to land the beauty it got off the hook and made a lively strike for the bottom. And quick as a flash my trusty gaff hook shot down after him and caught him near the tail and back into the boat he was lifted with a wriggle and growl, and you can't blame him either.

"A Little trial, a broadened smile, O trout, I call you mine."

And so it goes day by day.

Alice

Thursday June 24

"Oh, hum!" (Stretch and a yawn). It's 5 o'clock, old man, better get up and get your boots on and go out on the lake. It's a fine morning, be dad.

Better wake, daughter Alice. We'll go out to Siskiwit bay this morning and see if we can hook up some more.

Today is Steamboat day again and we must have a little shipment this time.

"All right, Dad, I'm coming." And so we go out at 6 o'clock and row, and row, and row, back and forth until we get an awful big empty space in our stomachs—oh for something to eat!

Ah! we catch a fine Kogefisk* and home we row for our dinner, and oh boy, if Ma was only with us now, wouldn't she, "mum, mum, mum," how good it tastes—right out of the water and onto the pan! That's eats for you.

Thar she blows! The steamer is in the channel. All aboard. And out we go—Alice, Edith, Magda, Lala, Elleanore,* Edward, Hans, Elling, the fish and everything.

Alice has the camera along and snap shoots the steamer also. Receives letter from Home—Smiles

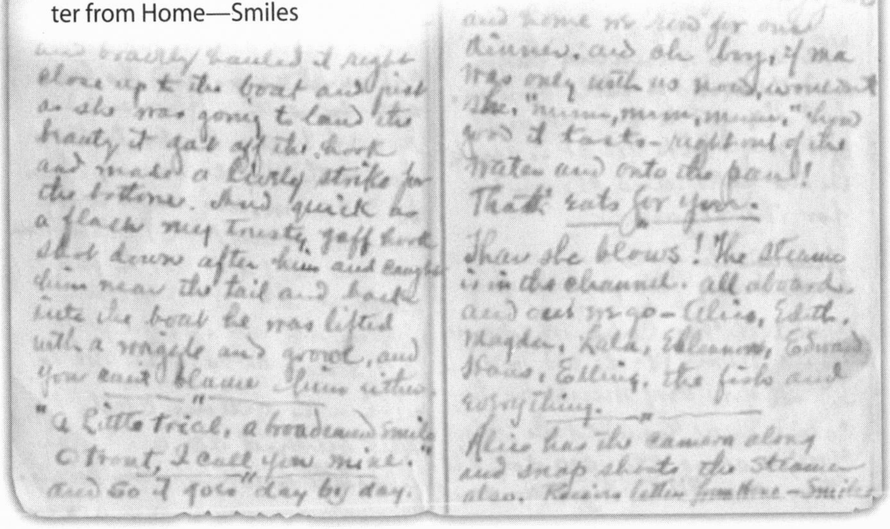

[handwritten manuscript reproduced]

and nearly hauled it right close up to the boat and just as she was going to land 'tis hardly it got off the hook and made a lively strike for the bottom. And quick as a flash my trusty gaff hook shot down after him and caught him near the tail and back into the boat he was lifted with a wiggle and growl, and you can't blame him either.

"A little tried, a broadened smile
O Trout, I call you mine."
And so I jog" day by day.

and home we row for our dinner, and oh boy, if ma was only with us now, wouldn't she, "mum, mum, mum," how good it tastes—right out of the water and onto the pan! That's eats for you.

Thar she blows! The steamer is in the channel. All aboard. And out we go—Alice, Edith, Magda, Lala, Elleanore, Edward, Hans, Elling, the fish and everything.

Alice has the camera along and snap shoots the steamer also. Receives letter from Home—Smiles

Friday, June 25

Just a year ago today Esther* caught the 29-pounder. Can we beat it to-day, Alice?

Fine morning, we'll go out to Redfin Island and wake up the big boys. But it was no use, the big boys are still out there. They saw us coming and hiked for safety, and we hiked sadly and hungry back to home with only 2 6-pounders as our reward. Oh well!

Home for dinner—a nice little dandy trout, with hot spuds and fresh bread and Java. It was an awful big cavity to fill up, but we went to it like heroes.

1 o'clock—wind east—increasing in velocity and we can't get out on the lake this afternoon

Set a net, which I loaned from Hans, last night. Wonder if there is any fish in it yet. If the weather moderates, I'll go out and see. Hans is a pretty good fellow.

5:30—just got through with our beautiful supper. Fish? No! Aunt Pajamas. Alice is getting to be an expert cook and also an expert dishwasher.

She can handle the oars and pull in the fish to perfection.

Her freckles are getting bigger now.

Saturday June 26

Rained all night—but I don't care; it didn't leak in my bed—I've fixed the roof. It leaked a little on the table, but what's the use of kicking.

Sea running pretty high this morning. Was out as far as the reefs, but the breakers were too high and I didn't like to take any chances going over the reefs.

11:30—Alice just rolled out of bed—pretty soft, I'll say—

She's now making flap jacks for herself. I've had my eats.

Listen to the hoarse fog whistles of the Ore Steamers about 30 miles out. Some fog out there.

"Don't eat so much!" shouts Mrs. E.T. as I stand outside my cabin chucking away a big slice of bread and a cup of coffee.

Well, Alice, shall we try and slide the reefs. The sea has gone down a bit. "All right, Dad," says Alice.

All aboard, the good ship "ALICE S." is speeding towards the reefs. Now let's lift the net and see if there are any "big boys" in it. Well, well, 5 Trout and 2 Lawyers.* That's pretty good.

Caught a nice 2-lb. Brooktrout for supper. And Alice made a dandy lunch.

Fried Brooktrout, hot spuds, tea, fresh bread, etc. Did we eat? Well, I'll say so.

Roses are red, but what do you suppose.
They are never so red as the tip of my nose
—Jerusha

Sunday June 27

A little more of the sam stoff! Rained nearly all night, with flashes of lightning and rumbling thunder. No fishing weather. Lake is too rough.

Shoreline photo by
Elling Seglem

A heavy fog is enshrouding everything this morning and a chilly raw wind is blowing off the lake.

10:30—Alice is still sound asleep. Just had breakfast by my loneliness. First 2 big dishes of rice. 2nd—2 cups of java with bread, butter and jelly, 3d—A big dish of hot oatmeal. That ought to hold me a while.

Hope you can make out this blotchy writing. Blame the paper.

Hans came over and had a cup of coffee with me.
Poor Hans.

Knockwood—No mosquitoes and no Black flies at Fisherman's Home. We don't want 'em anyway.

Invited to Edward's for Dinner but in the meantime we have Bacon and Eggs just to fill in with.

After dinner Hans and I and the girls took a trip in his boat to Little Siskiwit Bay.* A very pleasant trip of 10 miles. Alice enjoyed it very much.

Hans and I went to Redfin to troll. Out of luck.

Boiled trout, hot spuds, bread and tea for supper.

Raining—Good night.

Monday 28th

Steamboat Day

Got up early and went out on the lake quite early. Had pretty good luck. Started out at 7—back at 11. Lifted my net and got 12 Trout in it. And got 8 trout on the trolling hook—20 in all. If I keep on like that I am satisfied. Well, Ma, I wish you were here to get some of this nice fish. It's live under the knife. That's good eats, and so help me cheese and crackers. We eat it all the time. Well, so long everybody.   Ye Ed—

Elling with five good ones

Those of our readers who are interested in fish stories will do well to renew their subscription. And if they don't like the way it is gotten up they <u>can send us a $ and we</u> will stop sending it.

Fisherman's Home Journal

Fisherman's Luck – A wet after deck and an empty forecastle.

No. 3.　　　　ISLE ROYALE, MICH.　　Week Ending July 4th, 1920.

Monday June 28

AFTERNOON SESSION

Thanks, awfully folks for sending us all that nice candy and those interesting newspapers And letters.

Alice is all smiles now and you can't really blame her either.

That candy. Oh folks! It certainly tasted good. Way out here in the wilderness m–m–m!

Got some interesting pictures from Norway—from Esther's friend Edith.

The lake was nice and calm, but the weather some what foggy and the Steamer came kind of late on account of the fog.

Well, right away, I advertise for newspapers and right away I get 'em.

Ma says they have flop jacks at home—the disease must be catching

That Basement Blow out must have been some razzle. (Not jazzy?)

Go it, folks—go it—while you're young. The kitten plays a year and regrets it the rest of his life—Don't be a kitten—Be a live one.

Tuesday June 29

3 o'clock, A.M! Shall I or shall I not? I shall! By the crooked horn of the sacred goat, I will get up. That's all there is to it.

So up I come, first one foot, then the other. And out of bed I take a grand tumble.

Oh glorious nature, you are also awakening! I opens my Cabin door and is met with a chorus of hundreds of birds warbling their beautiful morning praise to their Great Creator from their tiny perches in the tree tops. It is soul–inspiring, it is great!

The warm, bracing morning air as the sun bursts forth its golden rays in the East puts new life and energy into my very soul.

And as I stands here in my cabin door enjoying these blessings a wild (yet tame) rabbit bounces out of the bushes by my feet and stops near me and wonders what kind of animal I am, whether friend or foe.

4 o'clock A.M. Hop in to my good ship "ALICE S." and out I go on the lake, gliding along on the mirrorlike billows like a duck.

Alice is not disturbed – she sleeps.

Sunrise on Seglem's Harbor

Wednesday June 30

"Alice, Alice!"—(calling again) "Alice!" She wakes and grunts. "Wha!" "Will you go with me on the lake this morning? (5 o'clock) It's a fine morning on the lake, come on along!

"All right, Dad, I'm coming!"

So we chuck away Bacon and Eggs, fresh bread and coff and a dish of my famous, beautiful rice, and out we go to Siskiwit Point and lifts our net. 5 Trout was in it. 'Twasn't so bad.

Trolled in to the Bay, picked up 5 Trout. Kin 'o skimpy.

Picked up a boat load of kindling wood and brought home with us.

Oh! Horrors! Went over to the cave and greeted my old friends, the skeletons.* Took a picture of them and bid them "So long, I'll see you later."

Barnum,* the Duluth millionaire, came into Fisherman's Home for a visit, in his swell launch the "Halcyon". Snapped it.

The day was Ideal, both on land and water.

Poor Alice—she likes to be sun–baked—and she's nearly roasted. She's as red as a lobster and tough as Esther.

Thursday July 1

Well, getting up at sun rise 3A.M. isn't such a bad stunt after all. Out on the lake at 4. Rowed 4 miles and was back home at 8 o'clock.

Lifted net but got only 1 trout and 1 Menominee.* Some "luck," I'll say.

I am now cooking Prunes. By heck they burned to the bottom of the pan. "More luck"

What do you know about that? My watch is on the bum—spring busted or guts dislocated.

Cleaned 16 fish. Shipped one to Thora* and had a nice Kogefisk for dinner.

I am so full of fish I can feel it stick out of my ears. Ooff!

A Northeaster is blowing up and it is starting to rain.

Alice is washing dishes. She is a pippin at that—it pays to advertise in the F.H. Journal.

Very rough on the lake. Strong N.E. blowing, with thick fog. Went out to meet Steamer and searched around for it a long time, blowing our fog horn all the time. Well, Suddenly she looms up a short distance from our boat. The heavy swells bounced us up against the Steamer's side like a cork.

Got newspapers, letters and groceries. Shipped 13 poor fishes.

Alice is sad— Reason—No mail for her—poor thing!

High seas

37

Friday July 2

Rough day on the lake, but a perfect Shore day with sunshine and warmth. Great for landlubbing.

My friend Hans & I hiked over to Boat Harbor* through the jungle, Hans as my guide—he knows the trail. He Keeps ahead of me and we get to an opening in the forest where we find delicious sweet strawberries, and we pick and eat as we trudge along. Finally I lose my friend in the jungle and before I know it I am hopelessly lost—swallowed up in the woods. I holler for Hans, but he is too far distant to hear me. I shouts to the top of my voice for him, several times, and then some, and at last I hear him feebly shouting back. Finally we come into communication again—and Eureka! We find each other. Some experience!

On the way back we pick strawberries and I bring home a canful of the dainty morsels to my dear Alice—

Hans Mindstrom

and lo! We have—yum, yum—Strawberries and cream, delicious cookies, and tea for supper along with fried brook trout and Hot Spuds, fresh bread and prune sauce. Some menu—Don't it make your mouth water when you read this?

Weather is moderating. I out to the point and hauls up 2 6–pounders.

Saturday July 3

3 o'clock and all is well—except the weather—wind blowing strong from the N. E. Went back to bed and slept till Alice woke me up—7 o'ck.

Alice cooks caffe and flop jacks and lets me lay in bed and snooze until she has 'em done—a big stack of Aunt Pajamas—oh boy! it's pretty soft to have a good cook—Pretty soft, I'll say! Well, I tumbles out o' bed and behold—the big stack before me on the table!

Great "Stoff"—if Ma could only see me now.

<u>Yes, they are good.</u>

Alice is now cooking a big pot of Dad's beautiful rice and between putting wood in the stove she is crocheting some beautiful things for the folks at home.

Alice Flipping Flop-jacks

E.T. ran a long rusty nail in his foot while chopping wood in the dark and today his foot is all swollen up. Moral:—Don't chop wood in the dark.

THEY ALL
FLOP SOONER
OR LATER!

Went out to the point to lift my net—4 Trout, 1 on troll. Wind and seas strong. Had to row back home right away. Aw, why can't the Weatherman behave himself?

Dad Flopping out of bed

This bum paper gets my goat—it's like blotting. Think I will have to use pencil after this. So the home folks can read what Ye ED. is trying to spell.

Nice boiled Trout for Supper—ah! that's feed!

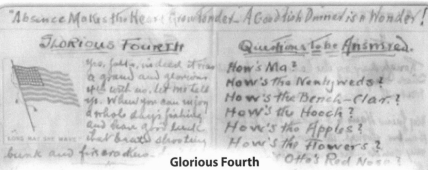

Glorious Fourth

Yes, folks, indeed it was a grand and glorious 4th with us, let me tell ye. When you can enjoy a whole day's fishing and have good luck that beats shooting bunk and firecrackers – don't it?

Ha, well I have to gurgle when I tell you (ha – ha) that Alice and Ye Ed had a great (ha– ha– ha) time pulling in 13 (ha – ha – ha– ha) big trout (oh-ho!) and she is not afraid (oh no) to grab 'em by the neck (No Sir) and yank the hooks out of them. She's a reglar pippin at it (you bet) and can take her seat among the hardiest fish dogs.

Everything is lovely and the goose's neck hangs low.

The pet (?) Squirrel had a regular picnic all to himself last night chasing in front of his tail up and down the side of my shack and over the roof. Wish I could catch the rascal. I'd fix his tail.

A rabbit tangled itself into the net, last night, that is, stretched around the potato garden and you ought to have heard how he hollered. Poor thing, he hung there when I came out. I released him and, by cracky, you ought to see the son of a gun run.

Questions To be Answered.

How's Ma?
How's the Newlyweds?
How's the Bench—Clar?*
How's the Hooch?

How's the Apples?
How's the Flowers?
How's Otto's* Red Nose?
How's Vera's* Corns?
How's Jennie's* Cold Feet?
How's Katz's Bumgalow?
How's Everything?
How's Bill's Heart?
How's Roy's* Ginnies?
How's Esther's Roughneck?
How's the Coal Bin?
How's the Gold Fish?
How's J. Barleycorn's Coffin?
How's the Birdlot?
How's yer Appetite?
How's the Journal?
How's Tanta's Rheumatism?
How's the Bear Cat?

That'll be Enough for this Time—S'long.   Ye Ed.

Questions to be Answered.

How's Ma?
How's the Newlyweds?
How's the Bench-Clar.?
How's the Hooch?
How's the Apples?
How's the Flowers?
How's Otto's Red Nose?
How's Vera's Corns?
How's Jennie's Cold Feet?
How's Katz's Bumgalow?
How's Everything?
How's Bill's Heart?
How's Roy's Ginnies?
How's Esther's Roughneck?
How's the Coal Bin?
How's the Gold Fish?
How's J. Barleycorn's Coffin?
How's the Birdlot?
How's yer appetite?
How's the Journal?
How's Tanta's Rheumatism?
How's the Bear Cat?
That'll be enough for this Time—S'long.   Ye Ed.

ADVERTISEMENT

WANTED

INVITATION

41

Fisherman's Home Journal.

WHAT IS HOME WITHOUT A FISH? – A DISAPPOINTED WAITER.

No. 4 — ISLE ROYALE, FISHAGAIN. — For the Week Ending July Eleventh 1920.

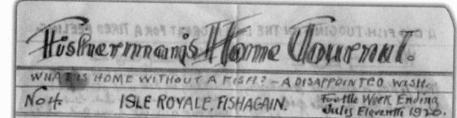

Monday, July 5th

"Well, well, if here isn't Old Friend Halloran again." "Where yo' goin' this morning?" "Just going to get my mail on today's steamer."

While out in Siskiwit early this morning I meet the old gink coming serenely paddling along in his little Irish-painted boat as happy as a lark.

E.T.'s foot looks pretty bad. He's going to Duluth on today's boat to see a doctor about it. Wise thing to do.

Well, E.T. went on the Steamer and had a hard job climbing aboard with his bad foot.

The girls went out to the boat too, with bouquets for the captain.

Old Halloran went with us out to the boat.

Had a pretty nice shipment of fish this trip. Hope to repeat it at the next trip.

Got mail from home and returned to our shack happy.

Fish heads for supper.

Tuesday, July 6th

"Say, Girls. What's the matter with taking a trip to McCormick's this afternoon, it looks pretty fair weather, eh?"

"All right Dad, you're on, old scout. To the McCormick's it is."

Alice, Edith, & Dad set out for the coveted place in high hopes of getting a few of the big whoppers that lurk around there, and reached the reef at 2 o'clock. We had barely got our hooks out when a stiff breeze from seaward blew in a heavy fog and we had to "hike" for land. We landed at Attwood beach* where we cooked coffee and had lunch. After which we filled our boat with kindling wood and I rowed for home without having a chance for fishing. I told Alice to put out the hook on our homeward journey as we might get a Koge fisk and sure enough we picked up four as we mosied along the rocky coast.

Back home at 6 o'clock. Felt pretty good. Not very tired although I had rowed about 20 miles that day.

A little more "of the same stoff"—Fish heads for Supper

Mending nets

43

A BIG FISH TUGGING ON THE LINE IS GREAT FOR A TIRED FEELING

Wednesday July 7th

Well to day is general wash day at this burg and the girls are busy rubbing and scrubbing <u>officer</u> at the wash tub.

Think I'll throw in my socks while the suds is bubbling. I don't know as they need a bath but I'll do it just for general principles.

The Old Girl tells us that Jennie is coming here on the next Steamer. Wonder if it is really so. Bless her Soul. We certainly would be delighted if she would come. And tomorrow will be the day. But it's too good to be true.

—Well, we'll see tomorrow

Went out to the rocks but with no success. It's funny, they seem to go way out in deep water (100 fathoms or more) when I come around—well, you can't blame 'em either—they want to live as well as myself!

That daughter of mine is getting to be a reg'lar ruffneck, by heck. And be sides she seems to lay on fat. Well, <u>go to it</u> kid. The ruff stuff is what you need.

Oh, man, but she can twirl the flapjacks! Good night!

Wild rose bushes are now in full bloom—and the blue bells, too.

Thursday July 8th

Say, old man (talking to myself), you can't lay in bed and stretch on a nice morning like this. Get up and out and get some fish while it's nice and calm.

Think I'll go down to the point, and see what luck I have there. Ah, Tain't so awfully bad, and a 2 1/2 Brook Trout for dinner. Oh, man and woman, Alice fried it and talk about feed! That's something we can never get in Chicago—Brooktrout.

Well, I'll have a little shipment for today's boat too, be dad.

Mrs. Seglem made a delicious cocoanut cream pie this morning and sent Lala over with half a pie for us, but when she got half way over to our shack she ran so fast that she stumbled and fell and smashed the pie on the rocks. Well, the chickens had a nice feast of it. Lucky chickens, I'll say.

Went down to Redfin but didn't get a smile, and had a deuce of a time coming back in a strong head wind and sea. Oh but my poor hands are sore from rowing.

Thar She Blows! Steamer is here! All aboard girls! Out we go to meet the boat.

OH! LOOK WHO'S ON THE BOAT! JENNIE!!!!

45

Friday July 9th

Well, Jennie stepped off the Steamer last night all right. Some surprise, I'll say, when she stuck her smiling face out through the gang way and squinted down upon us poor simps in the fish boat laying alongside the big Steamer.

Hurrah! for our new cook! Now we'll have real feed. Here you see her on the job already, fixing bacon and eggs—Oh, man, God blesser that she'd dare venture out here in the wilderness

Mighty glad she came, I'll say.

And you ought to see all the goodies she brought along—Well, it certainly was enough to make any crepehanger put a holiday mask on his face.

Beef! Oh boy! that new cook must have had an EX-ray picture of that awful cavity in our inner shambles, for she went on shore at Port Arthur and bought out a small butcher shop—a hunk of cow the size of young steer and we have been beefing ever since.

Ham and Eggs for Supper.

One of E.T.'s daughters, Alice and Jennie (standing)

Saturday July 10

Took the New Cook over to the cave and introduced her to our friends the Skeletons and they were mighty glad to meet her. Setting all gruesome jokes aside—she wasn't a bit afraid. Brave girl!

And Alice is no back number either, let me tell you—she had her picture taken holding the skull and cross bones.

Well, folks, this is the real life. Hans towed us (Jenny, Alice, Ye Ed. and a girl from Duluth) out to the rocks (Esther Krumm) and he went out on deep water about a mile away to lift a gang of nets. Took the Duluth yenta with him and we kept trolling on the reef for some time & then paid a visit to Hans' happy home at Boat Harbor, then to our happy Fisherman's Home

Took several snapshots and enjoyed the trip nicely.

Here's a Chance for Dalrymple*
"Talk about Wet and Dry," said Hans to me this morning. "You ought to see the fish when I got it out of the lake."

Well, good night folks, I'll see you in the morning.

Sunday July 11

"Eat 'em while they're hot" says our new cook. She's slingin' Aunt Pajamas this morning to beat the band, and do you know, folks, she couldn't make 'em fast enough. Not to exaggerate, yours truly eat at least 10, while Alice stowed away a round dozen. Poor cook, I don't know what she got, but she said, "Please pass the syrup."

So as to relieve the tension at Seglem's Restaurant we had dinner at E.T.s hotel to day.

MENU:
Fish

Got up at sunrise this A.M. Went out to the point. Caught 8 fish and was back before the girls were out of bed—Thas going some. I'll say!

"The Angel's Serenade" will be sung tonight at Seglem's Opera House by the Hummer's Concert Band.

Artists:
{Miss Mosquito, Soprano
{Mr. O.U. Sucker, Tenor
{Mr. I.M. Stung, Basso
{Miss How. I. Scratch, Pianist
{Mr. Will U. Slappem, Violinist

Concert begins right after supper. For enchores—slap yourself in the face. Admission Free.

Comments & Boasts

That currant jam Ma sent along with Aunt Jenny was simply delicious. Wish we had a bushel of it—

Seglem's Shack. 23 Fish Blvd.

Abe Olsen* is still on the job.

Alice is getting mighty fat and "sassy", I'll say.

Jennie seems to like it out here—at least she says so.

Oh, thanks awfully for the stamps. Your heart is in the right spot—old girl.

Thank you Esther for the poem you "rotten" on the "typerotter". What yo tink of the speel?

Hope the "Gang" had a lofly time at "My Indiana hoame" during the "shoating" days.

Best wishes and love to Russell Arch.* Welcome to our city.

Hope Mostar* is all right again. How's Manda?* Ye Ed.

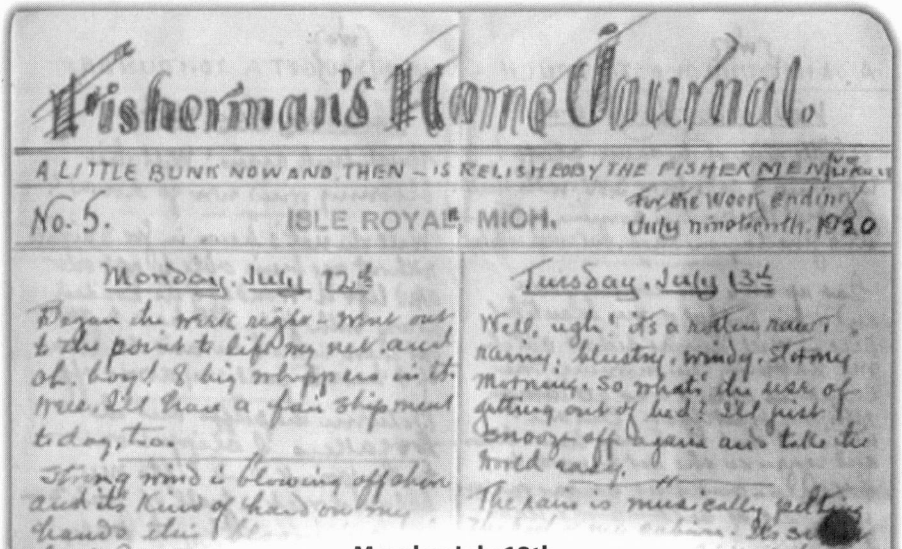

Fisherman's Home Journal.

A LITTLE BUNK NOW AND THEN — IS RELISHED BY THE FISHER MEN

No. 5.　　　ISLE ROYALE, MICH.　　For the Week ending July nineteenth. 1920

(handwritten journal entries for Monday July 12th and Tuesday July 13th)

Monday July 12th

Began the week right—went out to the point to lift my net, and oh, boy! 8 big whoppers in it. Well, I'll have a fair shipment today, too.

Strong wind is blowing off shore and it's kind of hard on my hands this blooming rowing but I got to put up with it.

Well, I'll row my head off as long as there is fish to get.

Went out to meet the Steamer with our fish. Hans takes care of the engine while Ye Ed steers the boat. The girls were along as usual and enjoyed a rough voyage in a choppy sea.

Here they are: Alice, Jennie, Edith, Magda, Anna, Lala, and Elenor— some bunch.

I think Jenny was a little scared as I noticed her eyes roll worse than the boat.

E.T. returned from Duluth with his foot fixed up by the Dr. but still it isn't well yet.

Received mail from home and returned to the shack happy.

Tuesday July 13th

Well, ugh! it's a rotten raw, rainy, blustry, windy, stormy morning, so what's the use of getting out of bed? I'll just snooze off again and take the world easy.

The rain is musically pelting the roof of my cabin. It's sweet music indeed— I like to listen to the big drops hitting the lid.

"Hey! wake up there!" shouts a squeeky voice into my cabin door. "It's 9 o'clock. Are you gone to sleep till the blood rots in you or what?"

"All right, Jennie, I'll get up, and that mighty quick," says I. "Flop jacks this morning, hey, Jennie?" "All right."

I jumps out o' bed and in a jiffy the fire is roaring and the coffee pot is singing on the hole.

Breakfast: Rice, Oatmeal, WE LIKE IT. Flopjacks and Coffee.

The bum weather keeps on all day and it's kind of chilly. The only thing to do is to keep close to the hot stove and hope for a better day tomorrow.

Good gracious, how we been eating today. Holy stomach!

Wednesday July 14th

A little more of the same stoff! Blowing a gale from S.W. with thick fog, but the sun is coming out and it's a fine day on shore, but rough on the lake.

Got up at 6 and cooked java and a big potful of my beautiful rice—Well Jenny didn't catch me napping this morning. She came in after I was all through with my breakfast. But she insisted that I should have bacon and eggs—so she set to work to fry eggs and <u>put sugar on 'em</u> instead of salt—some flavor I'll say.

Oh, inner man! The new cook is baking coffee bread and also rye bread today. Some cook, I tell you.

Here we have it, girls, go to it—it's good, even if I have to brag about it myself.

"Skrydt shelf, jug har inte ted,*" says Jennie.

Well, we like it, and Jennie says it's all right—so it must be for Jennie knows a good thing when she—tastes it.

The breakers are running high today, a very beautiful sight and music to see and hear them thundering against the rocky shore. Oh boy, it reminds me of my dear childhood days—home in Norway.*

[Handwritten journal facsimile: Wednesday July 14th and Thursday July 15th]

Thursday July 15th

Tough luck again! Will that blooming wind ever go down?

Well, the net's been in for 3 nights without me being able to get out and lift it. Wonder if it's loaded down with fish. I'll have to get out there somehow and see even if I have to pull my arms off.

Between the puffs and the breakers I slips out to the point and lifts my beloved net—full of fish? —Well, not exactly—only one poor forlorn "shark"—sharks are not all lawyers but all lawyers are sharks.

The "shark" I got was a "lawyer" or eelpouch, or "låke"* as the Swedes call them. Ma Knows.*

So we had "shark" for dinner. It had a nice big fat white liver and we boiled it. Oh boy! You ought to see Ye Ed and his beloved sisinlaw go after that liver! But Alice kept shy of it, Poor Kid.

Capt. Purdie* came paddling in here with a bum engine so Hans had to tow him home to Wright's Island 8 miles across the Siskiwit Bay. They started out right after supper and took all the girls along. I didn't go. They got back about 12 o'clock at night. They had a nice trip—so they all say.

BRAIN ON WATER IS A WHOLE LOT BETTER THAN WATER ON THE BRAIN

Friday July 16th

<u>You got to hand it to her,</u> I'll say. I tried to wake Alice about 6 this a.m. and she said "Grunt" and fell to sleep again.

I wanted her to help me get out and do some fishing—it was a nice calm morning with a warm sun up, but she slept on till I got back. The Lord knows what time it was. I don't like to tell for fear you might say "Gee Whizz."

Well, I caught six 8-pounders and chucked them in the Home Keg. A few more like that will soon fill it. Then Hallelujah!

By heck, what yo' tink! When Jennie made my bunk this A.M. she found a big tack with the business end up in my bed. Who's tryin' to murder me?

Caught another "shark" in my net to day. A big feller with a stomach like a Chicago Alderman. And you ought to see that fine white liver. Well, that lawyer will make a fine dinner tomorrow.

Wind is again blowing strong from the S.W. and we can't get out again to day—some luck!

Halloran went back home to Minneapolis yesterday. He left his boat here. The kids are using it on the bay.

Saturday July 17th

Cloudy morning with a S.W. breeze blowing. Got up at 6 and went out to the point. Got 1 trout in the net, but 0 on troll. Think I'll advertise for Jonah and throw him in the lake—maybe my luck will change, yes, no?

Well, Ye Ed's sisinlaw is baking swell bread today—bless her heart. I really don't know what we would do without her.

Aw, whadda ya' no about that? It's starting to rain again. Pouring down—it looks like an all day going. This would be a grand place for Dalrymple.

The dull rumble of thunder makes it kind o' cheery.

It is now blowing a gale from the N.E. The rain is pelting the roof of our cabin like hail. The fog is very thick and the sea beginning to run high.

Some weather, I'll say, but then on shore and in the cabin it is <u>pretty soft</u> —all you have to do is to lay in bed and push it out with your feet.

The girls are working hard on the "BUNK SHOOTER'S BULLETIN"—some document.

They are all squatting down all over the kitchen floor—it looks like a game of craps.

Really it's a game of "scraps." I had to cook a whole kettle of paste for them.

Sunday July 18th

Really, folks, I'm ashamed of myself. I laid in bed this morning till the Sun kissed my face. But, you see it's this way:—The storm of yesterday is still blowing and the breakers are thundering against the rocks—so what's the use of getting up?

Some storm, I'll say—but today it isn't raining—the sun is bright and warm, and it is a fine shore day.

10 o'clock—the girls are just getting out of their bunks and the coffee is ready for them.

I've had mine—2 cups—3 slices of bread, butter, and cheese, a big dish of oatmeal, and a hunk of cake. Don't want any more till noon.

We are invited to E.T. for dinnah, and you bet we'll bring along our empty bread baskets—that's a cinch.

Oh, Boy! Here, folks, you see Jennie after stowing away 9 fish balls, 4 spuds, 2 cups of coffee, 2 big slices of bread, gravy, a sidedish of stewed carrots and beans and topped with a piece of lemon cream pie.

Really you can't blame her for asking someone to help her from the table.

Weather is calming down toward evening. Took a row out to the breakers just for exercise. They still show ugliness.

Oh beautiful nature, thou art grand and glorious—The wild flower "garden" of Isle Royale is now in full bloom—the birds are warbling too.

Thank you

Ma—for your rich information about everything around the home burg. Hope you had a fine time at Viroqua.*

Clarence—Glad to see you're working hard at the bench. Too bad the Hooch* is all gone.

Edith—I rejoice in your happiness. May it ever be so. You're sure in luck. My regards to Hubby.

Esther—Sorry I had to trouble you with that long letter, but please forgive me this time. Hope you didn't weep when you read it.

Roy—You must be making lots of money seeing you've got a job working in the Mint. I wish I had a job like that.

A WORD TO THE WISE

Please take good care of those apples on the trees as we would like to see them when we get home. Have Esther take a snap shot of them so in case the boys make a raid on them we will have their picture anyhow. Regards from Alice and Jen. I thank yo. Ye Ed.

57

Fisherman's Home Journal

When you get a whopper alongside the boat and lose 'm—Wouldn't Jar You?

No. 6   ISLE ROYAL, MICH.   For the Week Ending July 25th 1920

Monday, July 19

Well, folks, to begin with I just want to tell you that the wolves* were howling around us last night—not more than a block away from our cabin—some: "yip, yip" "wow mow" "yauouoip!" Sounded very fascinating indeed.

Went out to the Point to lift my net and after picking up a 9-pounder, proceeded along and at the farther end, another big boy (must have been at least 15 lbs.) came along up to the boat but got out. I reached after the bird but missed him by the skin of his tail and he waved me pleasantly "ta ta" as he struck for the "deep blue." Well, folks, you never saw such disgusted gink like Ye Ed when I watched the whopper disappear. ⬅—*!

Alice, Jennie and Ye Ed. went out to the net again in the P.M. and a big "lawyer" was caught and as I was about to pull him in the ship the "shark" got loose and struck for freedom, but the old fool ran right back into the net and by skillful handling I managed to land the ugly brute.

I cleaned the big "fool" for supper. He had a swell big white liver and as I was congratulating myself on a fine meal, laid the liver on the fish house floor while I washed the fish, and when I came back to get the liver a gull had been in there and swiped it on me.

Was I mad? Ask the girls—I don't like to tell you any more about it.

The fish house

Tuesday, July 20

Turned out to be a swell day on the lake—the wind calming down in the P.m. to a dead blank. Well, it's about time the weather moderates: It's been bum long enough.

I "smoked" the girls out of the cabin this time—really got them to go with me without a murmur. Alice, Jennie, and Ye Ed took a trip out to the "Rocks," 2 1/2 miles S.W., to set a net and do a little trolling and just as we were about to haul in the line and row for home a big tug was felt and Oh! joy! a nineteen-pounder hooked on. Well, you ought to see the girls' faces crack peculiar surprising smiles when Ye Ed gaffed the beauty into the boat.

Tell John, did as he told me to do, pet him and kissim for him. Well did I pet the whopper? Well I guess I did. In order to make him behave in the boat I gave him a sonofagun of a whack in the head with my "binger" that's always ready for such occasions.

If I could only have got a hold of the sucker of a gull that swiped my liver he'd get the same petting.

"Oh, the dirty skunk!" exclaimed Alice as she stood down at the fish house, when a gull flew directly over her and "whitewashed" her hair, clothes and hands. Well, you can hardly blame her—those pesky gulls are nuff to get anybody's goat. Hundreds of them congregate here from morning till night. Hollering all the time—enough to get you nuts.

Wednesday, July 21

Well, it certainly seems as if the trolling season is about over and I'll have to hope I can get enough in my net to fill my keg. Got only a "Koge fisk" on troll this morning although the weather was ideal for the sport.

Alice and I went out to the Rocks but had very scant success, and got back home about noon.

Jennie is baking some of that delicious bread, cake, "Johnnie-Jump-ups," and lemon cream Pie—Yum, yum, smack, <u>sure!</u>

Oh! folks! Talk about a swell feed. We had fried Brooktrout for dinner—and you otto see us chuck it away. If Ma could only have been with us to get a <u>real fish feed</u> like that.

Jennie is all spruced up in her new light blue checked "Sunday-go-to-meeting" wrapper. Oh, man, if Osmond could only see her now!

Alice made some swell lemonade, and treated us to a nice cool Drink. We live <u>high</u> even if the temperature is <u>low</u>. I'll say we do.

5 p.m.—It's clouding up again and looks like bum weather is about to set in again. Well, if I had my keg filled I'd skip for a <u>better place</u>—Chicago.

The girls are waxing wild flowers and they sure are beautiful and wonder-ful as well—I mean the flowers.

Too bad I haven't got a gun with me so we could pop a "long ear" occasion-ally. Then we could have "<u>rabbit hash with dumplings</u>." "Longears" or "Cot-tontails" are plentiful here now.

Thursday, July 22

For the love of fish, look who's here! A duck in the net. Well, we'll have a duck dinner to day for a change.

"Dinner ready!" shouts our Cullinary Artist. Oh how the boarders yelled when they heard that dinner "bell."

Ye ED—Had to let out all his belt.

Alice S.—Had to roll it off on the grass.

Jennie—Held on to her Stomach for 2 hours afterwards.

Don't want anymore till 3 o'clock.

You said it, old girl. The only trouble with you is that you can't keep pace with our appetites.

"AY BAN COOK FOR TEN YAR IN ONE PLACE AN' NOT A KEECK KUM MY WAY."

The "gang" all went out to meet the Steamer and get the mail— Some mail—3 great big bundles of newspapers from home—Now we can read our heads off. Also a batch of letters—You Otto see the grin on the girls when they got those Peanuts.

Our cullinary artist asserting herself

Hans went home to Knife River for a short visit. Coming back Monday.

The girls took a row out on the lake after dark. It was calm and nice weather, but threatening clouds made their appearance in the N.E.

Friday July 23

A terrific Electrical Storm accompanied with a steady downpour of rain and strong wind passed over the Island during the night. Had to go down and pull ALICE S. up to a safer mooring about 2 A.M. and by strenuous pulls got her high and dry.

We Wheekahgo ginks are sure in luck—invited over again to E.T. for dinner—Well, it had Chicago beat by 700 miles.

Ye Ed threw away his belt and unbuttoned pants to make room.

MENU

Roast Pork (Gravy a la ooz)
Stuffing (Like "Mother's")
Fresh Bread   Stomach Cake
Tomato Salad
Water Melon   Hot Java

Dinner at E.T.'s

Alice S.—What she didn't eat, she wrapped up and took it home.

Jennie—Hasn't eat since and as yet don't complain of being hungry.

Too bad I couldn't secure that "Evenrude" in time to use it on my boat. It's too late now. It's all over with.

Wind eased up in the P.M. and I slid out to my net and picked up two nice trout for the keg.

The sunset is beautiful—ever changing in color from the hue of a thunder cloud to blood red and purple, violet, old rose, and yellow green. Some freak of nature. Wonderful to behold.

The Storm keep me awake half the night—and so did the Skeeters.

Saturday July 24

By heck, if I could get my hands on that pesky "Cottontail" that's making the blooming *@! ? X@ racket under the floor every night I would pull his dodgasted long ears off.

You'd think all the skeletons from the yonder cave were having a shimmy dance on the kitchen floor the way those rabbits are carrying on under the cabin every night.

Jennie baked some swell bread today, also a dandy 2-story lemon cake. Oh boy, it looks mighty good!

She had a reg'lar Kaffeslaberas* under the trees by the cabin and the whole Seglem bunch were prominently in evidence.

The Seglem girls, Alice, Edith, and Magda dressed up in overalls, blackened their faces with soot, and each with a hunk of Water Melon, together with Jennie dresed up as Aunt Jemima, stuffed as fat as a goose and with a big cake in her hand, had Ye Ed snap their picture. It will be a "bird" of a scene (if it turns out well.)

Those girls can certainly rip it up some. Everybody laughed, even Edward (who only smiles twice a year) had to laugh.

Put up a big swing for the girls and they tried it out. O.K.

The weather has been fine today. Rolled out at sunrise and went out on the lake after a couple of cup of java, bread, and a big bowl of oatmeal.

Have to switch off on "delightful" Oatmeal as my "beautiful" rice has been exhausted.

63

Sunday, July 25

Whadda yo no bout dat? I'm sunkissed again this morning—It's a nice day but nothing doing on the lake, so a fellow might as well take it easy.

Had a bad dream about big ugly spiders with long hairy legs letting them selves down on me—and did I holler? Well they heard me in the Hotel* next door.

And of course the rabbits had a jubilee under the floor again.

Got up at 9 and made coffee and flop jacks—those big fellows that spreads themselves all over the pan—fried in butter. Oh, Girls!

"Daylight in the Swamp!" shouts I in through the door of the hotel next door where the girls are sound asleep. "Flop jacks on the pan and if you want them red hot you got to cum quick."

"Show us!" says the girls, and out they came tumbling, one after the other—of course Jennie first—and it kept Ye Ed as busy as a cat on a tin roof to supply the demand for the shinplasters fast enough for their greedy appetite.

"Yes, they are good" says Jenny after stowing away—well, I won't tell you how many. So they must have been good.

Invited over to E.T. again for Chicken Dinner—they are certainly treating us fine. If Ma was only here to enjoy it! !

Caught another duck in the net and salted down the skin for stuffing. Hope to get it home O.K. this time.

Elling, Almida, Mrs. E.T. and E.T. with chickens (later date)

Thanks Awfully

Thanks Awfully

Ma—For letter received from Viroqua. Hope you had an enjoyable time out there. I don't feel like stopping over there. It's out of my way.

Edith—For those nice Peanuts you sent us. Some treat out in this wilderness. We all say.

Esther—For the "Humdinger" hat you sent along. But it came kind of late as we are leaving on the 2nd.

Clarence—Just the same—Ma says you sent me a letter lately but I haven't received it yet. Well, it's all right, any how, now it's a little too late now. Thanks just the same.

Roy—For your last letter from Walkertown. I suppose you're home now. Take good care of the apples till we get home.

Ed—For taking care of the garden. Ma tells me you are "farming" around the house in good shape. How's the strawberry patch?

Note—That watch you say you sent Alice some time ago hasn't come yet. Did you insure the package? Some of our mail is sent via Houghton, Mich. instead of via Duluth and gets here about 2 weeks behind schedule time.

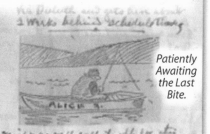

Patiently Awaiting the Last Bite.

Might as well call it off for this season. Trolling seems to be about over, so up with the line and back to good Old Chi.

There will be one more issue of the "Journal" before we set sail for the Southern Seas. Thanks for your fine 4-bearance. Ye Ed.

Fisherman's Home Journal

Best of friends sometimes must part — Farewell Beautiful Land of Isle Royale!

No 7.   ISLE ROYALE, MICH.   Final Edition — Week Ending AUG. 1st 1920

Monday, July 26

Well, folks, a week from today we'll kiss this beloved place a sweet farewell and hop aboard the good old tub "America" for Standard Rocks and the Blueberry Hill.

I'm feeling kind o' "chesty" this morning. We had a big bon fire again last night and the air was kind o' chilly around the blaze. Sounds strange, but it's a fact. Think I caught a little colt.

Nice morning on the lake. Had to help E.T. set out a mile of nets about 4 miles out-south of the Rocks, and we rowed all the distance in their little row boat—to save a few drops of gasoline, I think.

Hans went to Duluth last boat day and was supposed to come back to day, but didn't come. So E.T. can't do any net lifting without him. E.T. is sore at Hans. I suppose I'll have to help him out.

E.T.'s wife went to Duluth today for a short stay.

Caught a rabbit in the trap today and this evening we have rabbit stew (without dumplings) and a nice Brook trout on the side. <u>Some feed.</u> <u>I'll let you know.</u>

Got some of the pictures from Anderson.

Tuesday, July 27

I was up and out around the cabin before sunrise. But went to bed again. The air outside was calm and warm. Fell to sleep again and it was about 7 when I woke up.

Put on the coffee pot and took a squint at the weather—looks kind o' threatening.

7:30—Now it's pouring down and dripping from the leaky roof onto the table. Real fascinating.

8:00—The girls are pounding away on their ears—snoring to beat the band. Some sleepers, I'll say.

9:00—The girls are stirring a bit in the "hotel"—well, I have to put up some more coffee and have it ready for them when they come.

"Well, good morning, girls, are you really up and not weeping? "

"Want pajamas this morning?" says Jennie. "Got you sailing," says I. So flip, flap, fly, and the "red hots" are smiling at us. Such a delicious pile you never saw. "Go to it," says Jennie.

That Jennie girl is <u>some nurse</u> as well as cook—she put a hot stove lid on my weary chest last night and today I feel like fighting.

Alice (I think) got a letter from her friend Bill last night—she's all smiles this Morning.

Jennie and Alice on the bench

Completed the rustic bench so the folks can enjoy sitting out.

A Fisherman Must take his luck "philosophically" whether it's good, BAD, or wet.

A fisherman must take his luck philosophically, whether it's good, bad or rest.

Wednesday, July 28

Another severe electrical Storm passed over the Island last night and the vivid flashes of lightning were fierce, accompanied by deafening crashes of thunder, with a steady downpour of rain.

To day the wind is blowing a gale from the S.W. and the surf is churning the breakers against the rocks with thundering roar.

We are watching the monster combers as they madly hurl themselves in continuous performance in towards us on shore where the spray is drenching us if we venture too far out.

It is a grand and glorious sight to behold and the musical roar is indeed fascinating and wonderfully exhiliarating.

Fishing, as far as I'm concerned, is practically over. Tried it out before the wind blew up, but "O" doing. Not even in the net.

Will haul "Alice S." up and turn her over in a day or two and smear her bottom over with green paint. That'll stop her from leaking next summer.

"Supper ready," cries the cook.

The Sunset clouds are beautiful—black with a perfect silver lining—now they are turning a fiery red and purplish blue.

Thursday, July 29

Well, as the wind has gone down some I'll sneak out and haul up my net—it's full of big holes and tears from the storm and ripped beyond repairs.

The wind is now increasing to a gale and the sea is choppy.

This is the windiest season in many years. So say the old "fishhawks" around here.

"Where do yo' get that stuff?"
Well, folks, today is Wash Day and the women are busy at the tubs. I asked them to mop off one of my blue shirts but they simply refused on the ground that it was too <u>dirty</u> and <u>raggy</u> to face the soap.

E.T. and Ye Ed. went out to the Steamer in the skiff and rowed over the breakers, while the girls stood on shore and watched us "hump the bumps." Once in a while when we hit the high spots the girls would yell out "Oh, my!"

Hans came back from Duluth.

Had a little rain shower and a squall in the evening but it calmed down during the Night.

Got letter from <u>Clarence</u>, Ma, Ed, Hilda, Vera, Manda, Lillie,* also newspaper from Edith. <u>Thanks</u>.

Well, good night dear folks. I could tell you more, but I don't like to see you weep. —.

Friday, July 30th

This morning it is absolutely calm on the lake. I started out early and went down to the Point to see if there was anything doing. Rowed over the reefs a few times but without any success. So home I hiked without a nibble. No more this season on troll. Oh, well!

We'll just lay around and take the world easy until Monday. Then we shall kiss this ding busted place a long goodbye.

It's a very doubtful day. Sunshine + clouds. winds and calm, then threatening. Shall we risk a trip to Siskiwit Lake?

The folks are meditating: "Shall we" or "Shall we not?"—"We shall!"

2:30 P.m. —All aboard for Siskiwit Lake! Hans and Ye Ed., Alice, Jennie, Magda and Edith jumps into the big gas boat, and away we go—a distance of about 10 miles. The wind and sea being in our favor, and the lake smoothing down, made the trip a very delightful affair. The girls brought dainty sandwiches and a pot for cooking coffee on the shore. Reached our destination in about 1 1/2 Hours. Hiked 1/2 mile inland through the trail in the jungle and finally stood on the shore of the big placid body of water. Girls pulled off shoes and stockings and went wading up to their knees hunting green stones with fairly good success. Ye Ed also gave his feet a surprise by discarding his Brogans and dirty socks and went in after the green goods. Coffee and lunch were served and then the homeward journey started at 8 o'clock p.m. over a glassy lake and beautiful moon light.

Sunset on Siskiwit Lake
by Elling Seglem

Saturday, July 31st

6:30 g.m.—Got up and cooked coffee and <u>delightful</u> oatmeal—have to switch over to oatmeal as my <u>beautiful</u> rice has been exhausted.

The girls are still in dreamland and picking up greenstones in their sleep. Well, let 'em go to it, by heck!

It's a swell, warm, sunshiny morning and the little warblers are singing around the cabin. Too bad fishing stopped so soon. But such is luck.

10:00—"Did you really wake me up so early? Well, well, fine, fine."

Caught a nice big Brookie by the fish house and fried it for Dinner. We've done nothing but loafing and eating all day long. The time passes slowly when we have to do this land lubbing stunt, and we're counting the hours as they roll by until Monday when we shall say a tearful goodbye to this burg.

Had a nice sun shower this afternoon and us three Chicago ginks got caught in it while across the bay picking strawberries. But we should worry—we're no sugar lumps—we won't melt.

We are told in letters from home that the Masons are giving an excursion to Milwaukee on the Krixnix Kolumpus* today and that Ma is to continue her sporting proclivities and take hart and lunch and be one of the many to go along to the 2 1/2 percent City. Well, I sincerely hope that she may enjoy a very pleasant trip in nice weather. Have one on me, Ma.

Sunday, Aug. 1st

Ah, beautiful and refreshing morning. Clear and sunshiny, but a little Chilly breeze from the N.E.

A hot cup of coffee will fix me up fine. It's early and the girls are sleeping so I'll just have a cup all to myself.

Made enough of my delightful oatmeal yesterday morning to lap over to this A.M. so I'll just clean it up before the girls get here.

"Good morning, Girls. Will you have flopjacks for breakfast? Allright, they'll be right on your plates in a jiffy. Your last chance for a flopjack feed so you might as well choke down a few while the eating is good."

Gowan! Wadda yo' tink dis is a flopjack fact'ry?

Each one of us took a turn at the flopjack making. First Ye Ed., then the chief cook, and then Alice S. Then came the eating—Oh boy!

We are again invitationed to E.T. for dinnah—a real farewell chicken feed—and after lunch we are going to take a nice trip in Hans' big gas boat to Long Point—12 miles west of here along the coast. This will tap the joyrides for this summer and as the weather is ideal—the trip will be likewise.

All aboard! With flags flying the big choo-choo boat sticks her nose into the rough sea and westward we plow against a stiff wind and choppy sea for 12 miles to Long Point. Sometimes the boat would bang into a high one and send the spray all over us. It was fun—the girls liked it. When we got there, nobody were home.

Goodbye, Isle Royale!

Monday Aug. 2

Well, it is indeed with saddened heart we're packing up our few belongings today and taking a sweet farewell of this enchanting burg, where we have enjoyed our long stay. We certainly have had a most pleasant time among our own people and amidst the most romantic and strangely wild surroundings—both on land and water, and sincerely hope that we may be afforded another chance to visit this mysterious land.

To day is one of the finest days we've had since we came here and the bright warm Summer Sun is smiling down upon us and bidding us a pleasant journey.

All aboard for Standard Rock! Girls, jump in, the steamer is here. Goodbye, every body, thanks for every thing. Goodbye.

Well, so long folks—we'll see you later if not sooner. Ye Ed.

Goodbye, Isle Royale!
Monday Aug. 2.

Goodbye to the hillsides,
  Goodbye to the bay,
Goodby to our friends
  We are leaving today.
Goodbye to the woodlands
  And rocks on the shore,
Goodbye for perhaps
  We'll see you no more.

Goodbye, dear Isle Royale
  And Fisherman's Home;
With mem'ries so pleasant
  We homeward will roam.
When westward we're sailing
  With saddened heart
We'll always be singing,
  "Friends sometime must part."
          Ye Ed.

Alice and Elling

73

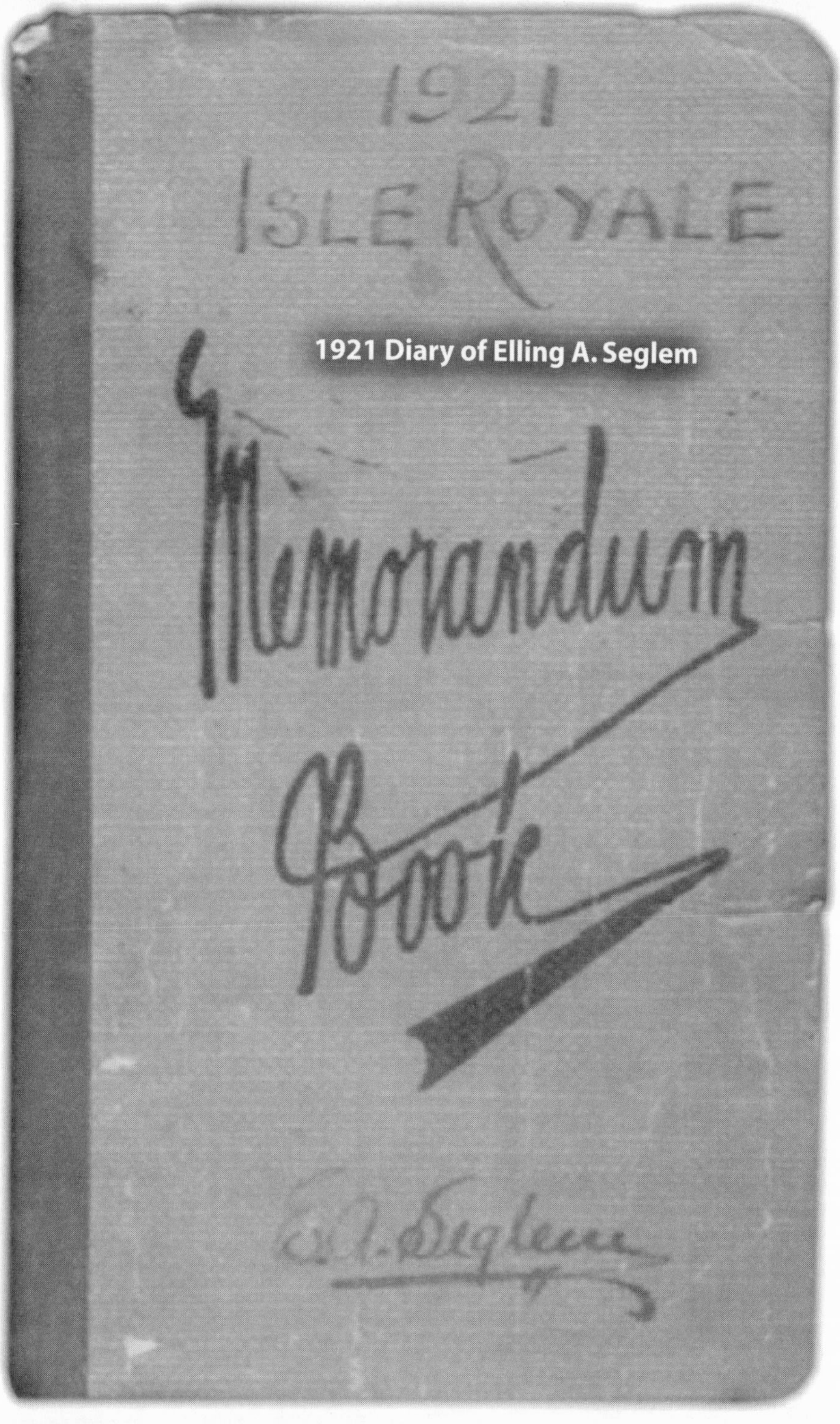

1921
ISLE ROYALE

1921 Diary of Elling A. Seglem

Memorandum

Book

E. A. Seglem

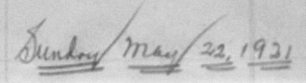

Sunday May 22

After having had a grand good time down stairs last night and a somewhat bum sleep got up early and prepared to get ready my duds for the trip. The "bunch" are gathering now in the evening again to bid the old scout good-bye. They are singing and having a fine time in the yard. The firlings* take me and the old girl to the depot and I'm off for the northland. Train leaves 10 p.m. on the NW. The heat and dust in the train is pretty tough, but the going is fine with no sleep.

Monday May 23

No sleep on the train all night. Got off the train at about 8 o'clock in the morning and made beeline for the lunch counter at Eau Claire, Wisc. Slop-water coffee, sinkers and apple sauce—some "breakfast" I'll say. Changed train for Duluth. Reached D. at 1:55 p.m. Had lunch. Went to see John and Gertie.* Then up to E.T.'s house.* Mr. Melby* and the Seglems came over and we had ice cream and lunch. Well, I'll tell the world I felt begrimed when I got off the train—dust, dirt, and cinders—well, give me a boat ride and you can have the train all to yourself. Hit the hay about 10.

Tuesday May 24th

Well, well, today is my birthday. First time I've been away from home on my birthday for 41 years. Order my provisions and other stuff but too late for the boat so I'll have to stay over until Sunday. Don't like that no how. I feel pretty good today after a good night's sleep. Put oil on Thorvald's* boat—he leaves tonight for the island. John* takes the bunch out riding in his car—went to Morgan Park*—got back to E.T. at 10:30. Too bad I couldn't get my stuff ready for tomorrow's boat. But still I have lots of time to get there.

Wednesday May 25

Had a good night's sleep. Gets up 7:00 and packed up my blankets and bedding ready for shipment. Went down to steamer dock* and greeted some of the officers on the boat, namely Chief Engineer McMillan, Steward Wallin, Purser Clausen, George Woodridge, and some of the boys in the steamer office. They were glad to see me again. Had lunch and took a car ride to Lester Park* and am now writing this sitting close to the lake at Lester Park. Nice day but it looks like rain. Went up to Pete Skadberg* and had supper there.

Thursday May 26th

A very chilly, raw, rainy day and I don't think I'll go out. This is my 33rd Wedding Anniversary—first time I've been away from the old Girl on the 26th of May since we were spliced. Wrote her a long letter. Met Thorvald from Standard Rock.* The women asked me to go along to the school entertainment but I declined with thanks.

Almida Seglem (Elling's wife) on a later trip

Friday May 27th

This is a bright morning so I better get up. 2 cups of java—2 eggs—2 slices of bread and cheese, well, it'll do. Went down town at 10 o'clock and met Thorvald from Standard Rock and bummed around until the afternoon. Had chop suey and took in a bum show. Invited over to Mr. Melby's in the evening. Could have gone with a party to Pike Lake* in the evening, but did not care to be bumped for 30 miles.

Saturday, May 28

A fine hot day. Broke the crystal of the watch and had to get a new one. 35 cts. gone. Hopped on the car and went to Morgan Park and New Duluth and the steel plant at Gary.* Took two bundles of luggage down to the steamer. Went up to see John Skadberg in the evening and he took me home in his Ford over the boulevard overlooking Duluth—a wonderful trip.

Sunday May 29

It rained all night and I thought we'd have a rough day on the lake but it calmed down nicely and at 10^{15} a.m. we started for Isle Royale on Str America. Thorvald Midbrod was in my company and got off the boat at Standard Rock. Lake very smooth but cloudy weather prevailed. Got into Grand Marais at 8 o'clock. Went to bed early and had a good night's sleep. Thunderstorm during the night.

Monday May 30

Steamer pulls into Fort William, Ontario* at 4:30 a.m. Stiff breeze blowing from the east and lake begins to get a little choppy. Arrived at Port Arthur, Canada* at 6 a.m. Mailed letter from there. Started for Isle Royale at 8 o'clock and arrived at Belle Isle* about 11, Tobin* at 1 and Rock Harbor at 2. On acc't of fog had to take the outer passage around Menagerie Light.* Arr. at F.H. at 5:30. Very cold day.

Tuesday May 31

Painted the bottom of my boat and fixed up my "duds." Fixed up the engine and tried her out on Thorvald's dory. Some humdinger of engine—sent the boat along at a six mile clip. Had fish dinner at E.T. Took a row out to the point in Halloran's boat and tried out the trolling but no luck. Too early in the season. Had a good night's sleep. Nice warm day.

Wednesday June 1

Got up at 8 o'clock and made breakfast which slid down the "gang plank" pretty swell. Windy and a choppy lake. Chilly. Cleaned out the shack in the woods and started to fix it up. Olaf* kind of peeved on account of having to remove his nets and other paraphenalia. O & E.T. had a set to on acc't of the ownership of the shack.

Thursday June 2

Wrote letter to the folks at home. A chilly foggy day. Went out with George* to Siskiwit Bay. Met the steamer in a driving rain.

Friday June 3

Worked all day fixing up my happy home and it's a dandy. I'm as snug as bug in a rug. Got a dandy little cook stove from the steamer. Made beautiful rice and lemonade. Feel like a King in his castle. Put out the boat and took a little row. Tette some potta.*

Saturday June 4

Went over with George to Boat Harbor and borrowed Hans' lamp and some dishes. Tried out the 'concrete mixer' again and it works to perfection.

Sunday June 5th

Went to Rock Harbor to pick Green Stones. Had a swell trip—got back about 6 p.m. and had supper at E.T. and it certainly slid down the "gang plank." Got a beautiful bunch of black fly bites at Rock Harbor.

Monday June 6th

Started fishing—went down to the point and tried it out—caught 2 in the forenoon and lost 2. Went home for dinner and afterwards cleaned the two fish and turned them over on my "oil acc't" to E.T. 7 lbs. Went out again at 5 o'clock and caught 5 nice trout. Got letters and card from Ma & Esther—sure glad to hear from home. Wrote 27 postcards. That's enough for one day.

Tuesday June 7th

Got up at 5 a.m., cooked coffee, had breakfast, oatmeal, coffee, bread, butter and prinost and oatmeal crackers. Started for the bay immediately after breakfast. Caught a 14 pounder and 3 smaller ones and lost 3 or 4. Wind started to blow and I "hiked" for home about 10. Had a big roast beef dinner at E.T.'s. Fixed up the flag staff and secured it to the shack and hoisted the Stars and Stripes—she looks pretty nifty. Geo. took picture of me in the doorway. Had a big supper of redfin and hot potatoes and coffee. Cooked a big pot full of beautiful rice. E.T. brought over 1/2 dozen eggs. Me for flapjacks.

Wednesday June 8th

As the wind was blowing a fresh breeze with thick fog overhanging the sun, I didn't get out of bunk till 8 a.m. Fried an egg, cooked coffee and had breakfast after which I went out to the bay, but nothing doing. Went as far as Francis Reef.* Wind started up again and I rowed for home. Had coffee can along and had lunch in the bay. Fish dinner at home with bread, butter, cheese and rice, coffee, etc. Felt tired after rowing continuously for 5 hours. Wrote several letters—took it easy. Had big fish supper.

Thursday June 9th

Foggy, windy morning but wind moderated and I went to the bay trolling but didn't have any success. This is steamer day so I cleaned what fish I had—8 in all—and shipped them—25 lbs—first shipment. Got letter from Ma telling about Mabel's wedding. Was at E.T. for dinner—had baked whitefish and it was mighty good. Cooked a big trout head for supper. Mailed 29 pieces of cards and letters.

Friday June 10th

Foggy, raw morning—got up at 5 and put on the coffee pot and went to bunk again. Woke up at 8 and had breakfast. Put name on my "Wooden Lizzie" and she looks nifty with her new name—ALMIDA. Some classy name for a boat. The little birdlets are out of their eggs. Gathered swell bouquet of wild flowers for my table. Made some delicious flopjacks.

The Almida on Chippewa Harbor

Saturday June 11th
Was up at 5, had breakfast and went to the bay but the north wind began to blow and the bay got very choppy. Caught 1 trout. Mosied back home and after lunch rowed over to Boat Harbor—caught 2 Tr. Rowed back home and had "Kompa"* for dinner at E.T. The wind shifted to a SW breeze and died down. Rowed back to the bay and caught 8 Tr. Got a tow home from Thorvald & George. Cooked a swell cup of coffee and had lunch. Felt kind of tired after rowing nearly all day.

Sunday June 12
A very blustry, windy day—tried out trolling but the wind increased to a gale and I had all I could do to get back home. Thorvald and George went to Redfin Island to troll but the weather was so rough they could do nothing. Got one measly fish in Siskiwit Bay.

Monday June 13
Another windy day. Tried out trolling early in the morning but nothing doing and the wind increased to a young gale and I hiked for home. Mrs. Seglem went to Duluth. Got letter from Edith. Fish head for supper. Felt A1 and very contented. Sent to John for a priming plug.

Tuesday June 14th

Out trolling for a little while but as wind increased and not much doing I rowed home again. Was out to the Rocks and in the bay. Caught 3 trout between Boat Harbor and Fisherman Home and one in the bay.

Wednesday June 15

Windy, stormy day and nothing doing on the lake. Made a stool from a sawed off log about a hundred years old according to the rings in it. It makes a dandy addition to my fancy furniture. Shot rabbit in the morning and skinned and cleaned it and boiled it. Will fry it in the morning.

Thursday June 16

A very fine warm day both on shore and on the lake. Tried out trolling in the bay but nothing doing. Went to Boat Harbor with George. Had rabbit steak for dinner. Took pictures of overturned tree. Helped Olaf push out his big fishing boat in the evening and got chewed up by mosquitos. Got letters from Alice, Esther and Roy.

Friday June 17

Got up at 5—made breakfast—coffee, bread, butter, cheese and rice—filled up pretty solid. Went out to the bay as it was a very fine morning, and trolled to the bottom of the bay—got 2 trout. Heavy fog set in so I mosied home towing the fish alive. Foggy all day—very thick. Rowed over to Boat Harbor trolling back and forth but nothing doing. Flop jacks for supper.

Saturday June 18

Woke up early but didn't start out until about 9 'oclock on acct' of fog. Shot out to the channel and caught 7—one a 33 1/2 pounder, others from 16, 14, 12, 10, 8, down to 3. got menominee from Gull. 4 in pm. —big fellows. Foggy all day off and on. Went as far as Redfin. Well, it's a pretty fair day—got 12 all together.

Sunday June 19

A very foggy disagreeable day. Got up about 7 'oclock had breakfast and attempted to go out trolling but the fog was very thick and I did not want to risk getting away from shore. In the p.m. fog lifted a little toward evening and I rowed out to the channel and caught 2 big fellows—one 16 pounds and one 15 pounds. Then the fog came rolling in again and I had to skip for the harbor.

Monday June 20

This is boat day. Went out trolling and caught ten,—two 21 pounds each—in the channel. Some fish, I'll say. Received letters from Alice, Abe and Axel. Received bolts from Clarence. Films from Duluth and lamp wick. Had a beautiful shipment of fish. 175 lbs. 10 big whoppers. Halloran came off the boat. Aunt Pajamas for supper.

Elling and Halloran

Tuesday June 21

Another foggy windy day. Went out to the bay trolling but wind got so strong I had to quit and Thorvald and George picked me up and towed me after they had towed old Halloran and his green skiff into his landing at the bottom of Siskiwit Bay. Clamped the engine on the skiff and tried her out, but after trying to troll with engine on the skiff, found it impractical and took it off again.

Wednesday June 22

A very windy day. The sun poured down its hot rays on the shore which made it a nice shore day but the lake was rough and no fishing weather. Had a little nap in the afternoon. Had flop jacks for dinner. Wrote letters to Clarence, John, Axel and Falk.* Post card to Ma. Took it pretty easy as getting out on the lake was out of the question.

Thursday June 23

Got up at quarter to 3 a.m. and cooked coffee. Had bacon and eggs and oatmeal, two big slices of bread, butter and cheese for breakfast. The morning being calm and warm, went out to the reefs at 4 a.m. but the wind of yesterday had chased the fish away. Rowed into Siskiwit Bay and caught 3 trout. Rowed out to Redfin but nothing doing. Home at noon. Made flopjacks again. Got spark plug from John. Received mail from Ma telling of departure for St. Louis with Esther, and letter from Alice, Irene, Aleck and Edwin.* Olaf came here from Knife River on way to Siskiwit Bay.

Friday June 24

Went to bed last night at 7 and got up this morning at 7. Some sleeping. Well, I feel pretty good just the same. Wind is blowing a gale from the east and the lake is very rough—out of the question to go out this morning so I'll take it easy. Had 2 cups coffee, 1 big slice of bread, butter and cheese, 5 flapjacks, oatmeal crackers and pear sauce for breakfast.

Saturday June 25
Started out to McCormick Reefs with my Evenrude and it ran OK all the way out (8 miles) but couldn't get it started going back and I had to row all the way against a strong wind. Nearly all in when I got back to F.H. at 8 p.m. No fish on the reefs.

Sunday June 26
Took a trip across Siskiwit Bay to Hay Bay* and visited Obert and Hansen,* also Bjorvek* and Lively. Took pictures of boys in the boat. Also of the Game Warden.

Hay Bay

Monday June 27
Big thunderstorm broke out at about 9 o'clock a.m. Was out trolling and barely got in the harbor when the storm broke out. After storm was over I went out on the lake again and caught a few fish. Judge May from Detroit came off the boat and was taken in to the bottom of Siskiwit Bay to Halloran's landing. About half doz. fellows came along bound for Halloran's cabin. Edward and Thorvald took the bunch in with their gas boat. I took their picture.

Tuesday June 28
A most perfect day both on land and water. Was out trolling nearly all day but got only 6 fish—some luck! Oh well, let's hope for better. The heat in Siskiwit Bay was so fierce I couldn't get in there to troll, although I tried it several times but had to turn back. I never felt the heat so bad on water. I'm all burned up.

Wednesday June 29

Another fine day for fishing. Very hot but a little more windy than yesterday. Had flopjacks and rice for breakfast. Was on the lake nearly all day. It turned out to be another beautiful hot day and I had to row along in my undershirt. Lost a couple of dandy fish but caught 13 good ones. This means good luck.

Thursday June 30

Went out trolling at 6 and got 5 nice trout—back at noon and had dinner and then cleaned fish for the boat. Shipped 24 fish—76 lbs. Mrs. Seglem and Edith came off the boat. The darn oil stove nearly smoked me out last night and it took me an hour this morning to clean up the dirt. Another hot day—hope the weather keeps up. Got letters from Ma, Esther, Ford, and card from Kock.

Friday July 1

A blustry, stormy day and bad on the lake—the wind being from the SE kicked up a choppy sea. I took it easy, confining myself to my cabin all day writing letters, eating, sleeping and washing clothes. Was over for dinner—beef—to E.T.'s.

Saturday July 2

A windy day—wind from the NorthEast but nice and warm. Was out trolling a little in the morning, rowing against a choppy sea and fresh breeze. Caught 4 trout, one little Kogefisk, just right for a big feed. Cooked it for dinner and eat the whole fish. Out again a little in the P.m. and caught 6 nice fish. Wind and sea pretty tough on my arms but otherwise I enjoyed the sport.

Sunday July 3

Well, I had a pretty fair night's sleep. Got up at 6 o'clock and had a big breakfast of Bacon & Eggs, Oatmeal, Bread, Butter & Jelly and two cups of java. Then out on the lake trolling. Had pretty fair luck—picked up 10 trout—Not very big—biggest 10 lbs. The day was a mixture of Sunshine, Fog, Wind and Calm with a strong current in the lake.

Monday July 4th

Well, on the previous 4th of Julys when I've been here I've had pretty good luck fishing but today luck was against me—I got only 4 trout. The weather was nice in the morning but suddenly the fog came rolling along and a gale from the SW blew up. Was in the bay and got a tow home from E.T. Got letter from Clar and 2 from Alice, also cards from Jack and Carson. Had fish heads for supper. Shipped 23.

Tuesday July 5

This is my lucky day. Broke the record and caught 32 fish. One a 16 pounder and one a 13 pounder. Out on the lake all day. A very fine day and calm.

Wednesday July 6

Out part of the day and caught 12. The fog made it somewhat bummy and I had to keep to shore.

Thursday July 7

Out a little in the morning and caught 6 nice trout. Had a dandy shipment—125 lbs. Judge May went home. Got box of swell candy from Edith. 2 letters from Ma, 1 from Downer, 1 from Irene, 1 from Jennie, 1 from Vera. The candy just touches the right spot.

Friday July 8

A peculiar foggy and sunshiny day. Was out to the rocks twice and combed the reef several times—caught 5—one a 14 pounder and a 10 pounder. Lost some big fellows. Had 'em up to the boat but they roughed off the hook and wagged their blooming tail at me as they made for the bottom. Well, such is a fishermans luck—Darn it.

Saturday July 9th

Got up 6 o'clock and made flapjacks and prepared to make a start for the fish hole. Nice calm morning but foggy. Started out at 7 o'clock for the rocks. The lake was the calmest I've seen it—absolutely still—not a ripple. Caught 20 nice big fish and lost 2 whoppers. Got back home at 6—out all day. Had lunch along—flopjacks and beautiful rice, bread and butter and milk. Felt kind o tired. Had supper at E.T.'s. Boys went to Washington Harbor.

Sunday July 10th

During the night a SW gale blew up and lasted all day, so I couldn't go trolling and I took it easy on shore. A nice warm sunshiny day—not hot—a real pleasant shore day. Invited to Seglems' for dinner. Roast duck—swell feed. The Washington Harbor party—Thorvald, Edith, Olaf and Julius* came back about midnight.

Monday July 11th

Got up at 4:30, had breakfast and as the morning was fine I went out on the lake at 6 o'clock and dropped the hook. Trolled from Fishermans Home to the rocks and the shore and was back at noon with 13 nice trout—one a 10 pounder. Had a severe attack of lumbago—the worst pain I ever had. Rubbed my self with Sloans when going to bed. On acc't of my back I couldn't make supper, so E.T. came over and asked me to join them. Had to stand up and eat alongside the woodpile. The Halloran bunch went home—one took picture of me and fish. Got papers from home, also letter from Edith, Clarence, Roy and Alice.

Tuesday July 12

Had a bum night with that sore back and didn't get up until after 7 o'clock when E.T. came over to inquire about me. Laid around and took it easy to get my back ache relieved. A swell warm day but I didn't go out until about 2 in the p.m. Was over to E.T.s for dinner under the trees in the park. Went out trolling about 2 p.m. —caught 7 trout—one a 16 pounder. Fish head for supper.

Wednesday July 13

Out trolling a little while and caught 10 trout.

Thursday July 14

Recieved letter from Ma and two from Esther and check from the U. and letter from Edith. Was out trolling in the morning and caught 11. Cleaned my fish for the boat and shipped 26 fish. Mrs. S. made ice cream—she sent Lala over with a big dish of it and it was swell.

Friday July 15

Well, this is a kind o' lazy day—didn't get out 'till about 7 o'clock. After breakfast I went out a little while and caught 7, but the wind blew up strong and the lake got choppy so I drifted along with the wind and sea all the way from the Rocks and got home and had lunch and laid down resting up.

Saturday July 16

Got up at 6 A.M. and made a big breakfast of bacon, eggs, oatmeal, fresh bread and coffee. Then E.T. took me in tow out to the Rocks where I trolled for some time and got caught in a fine little rain shower. Landed on the Rocks and rested awhile. Got back home about noon and after dinner took a nap and was woke up at 3 o'clock by my friend Halloran. Went out again trolling at 4—caught 9 trout altogether. Made a bunch of flappers for supper.

Sunday July 17
Big rain storm in the forenoon. Went to Long Point in the afternoon. Got back at 10 o'clock.

Monday July 18
Had a small shipment. Got letters from Ma, Alice.

Tuesday July 19
Fishing is getting poorer—got only 4 trout.

Wednesday July 20
To McCormick's reefs—got two 6 pounders and lost a big whopper—got one little Koge fisk at the Rocks.

Thursday July 21
This is my lucky day—no, I didn't get a bite (of fish) although I tried it out all over the reefs and in the bay. Had a very small shipment—Just 4 four-pounders. Received a big bundle of newspapers from home and a box of delicious cookies from Edith and letters from Ma, Esther, John, Alec and Margretha.* That's going some.

Friday July 22
Just two months today since I left good old Chi for this blessed place. A stormy day, with rain and a strong south west wind and heavy sea. Took it easy and "hit the hay" in the P.M. Had a fine beef dinner at E.T. Made a stack of flopjacks. Wrote letter to Edith.

Saturday July 23
Got up about 6 and went out trolling although it was a windy morning and caught 5 trout. Went to Halloran's in company with Thorvald, Olaf and Julius. Got to Halloran's about 7 o'clock. Had a fine tramp through the wood and ride across the little lake on the raft. Took a plunge and staid at Halloran's over night.

Sunday July 24
Well, I am at Halloran's cabin. Had a fairly good night's sleep. Had break-fast of bacon, potatoes, bread, coffee and dried peaches. Staid till about

11 o'clock then started homeward across the little lake on the rafts and got across in about 20 minutes and tramped through the woods to the big lake,—reached it at 12:15. —caught in big rain on way home— got to Seglem Harbor 1:15. Had dinner at E.T. Very novel interesting trip—found Moose Horn.

Rear to front:
Halloran, Elling, Julius Hanson, Olaf Seglem

Monday July 25

Well, I had a shipment of 10 trout but the lousy bums on the steamer only gave me 15 pounds for it—cheating me out of 5 lbs at least. Was out trolling in the morning and caught 5 small ones. The game is about over. Gertie came off the boat. Hans came to Boat Harbor.

Tuesday July 26

Out trolling a little while and caught 2 "kogefisk." Turned out to be a stormy day—big nor'easter with heavy sea and continued rain. Kept in and took it very easy all day. Had a big fish dinner. Speedboat passed.

Wednesday July 27

Stormy day and nothing doing on the lake. So I kept myself comfortable by sticking to my cabin. Rained pretty nearly all day. Wrote letters to Ma, Esther, Alice and Mrs. Williams.

Thursday July 28th

An ideal day with sunshine and nice warm weather. Went out trolling but with no success—not a bite—the trolling is now at an end. Went out to steamer with the boys and received my mail. Letter and pictures from Ma, letter from Esther, card from John and Minnie, letter from Roy. Had fish head for supper. Edith brought me hunk of rhubarb pie and it was delicious.

Friday July 29th

Got up at 6 o'clock and put away 2 cups java, 2 eggs, 4 slices of bacon and 2 big slices of bread, also a big pot of beautiful rice. With a small breeze from the SW I went to Boat Harbor with Hans' dishes—trolling as I went along. Went out to the rocks and about a mile west of the Rocks caught 4 trout. Wind increased and I had a nice time going home coasting along with the wind and sea. During the evening a storm set in.

Saturday July 30

The wind is blowing a gale from the SW and old Lake Superior is in an uproar. The reefs are breaking mountains high and it looks pretty ugly out seaward. E.T. and Thorvald tried to lift in the Bay but were forced back. Game Warden got as far as Sand Bay but couldn't get over the reefs so they turned back to Siskiwit. Wind now strong from NE and the day has been a blustry one but nice and warm. I've been taking it mighty easy today. Glad to stick around the shore. The wind is turning to north and it's getting cold.

Sunday July 31st

The folks went to Washington Harbor. I didn't go along as it looked like a doubtful day. Poured down in the afternoon. Went out trolling but didn't get anything. Kept to my cabin most of the day.

Monday Aug 1

Went out trolling and caught 5 trout. Sent my last shipment of fish—18 pounds. Went with E.T. out in the channel to set nets. Had chicken supper at E.T. and ice cream.

Tuesday Aug 2nd

Went over to Hay Bay to see Lively about engine but he had gone to Washington Harbor and would be back by Thursday.

Wednesday Aug 3

A very fine warm calm sunshiny day. Went out to the reefs, to the Rocks and to McCormick's reef—got 3 small trout. Halloran came down from his cabin on his way home by tomorrow's boat. "Concert" by "Pete and Ole" at Seglem's shack. Fish faces for supper.

Thursday Aug 4

There went the d___ old boat to h___ and I should have been with. Halloran went on the boat, so did Gertie. Got letter from Otto. Took picture of "Stella.*" Took pictures of Gulls and then "Stella." A remarkable fine day, got up at 8 o'clock a.m., felt kind tired after that long row yesterday. Edith brought me a slice of Water Melon. Fishheads supper.

Friday Aug 5th

Woke up about midnight by the hideous howls of the wolves prowling around cabin. A gale from the SSW blew up during the night and ruffled up the lake. Took pictures of breakers.

Saturday Aug 6th
A very stormy day. Trip to Siskiwit Bay. Reefs breaking.

Sunday Aug 7
To Hay Bay

Monday Aug 8
Left Fishermans Home

Fare RR	18.25
Fare SS	21.38
Fare RR	18.25

Exp. F. H.

E. T. Eggs. 6 doz.	1.80
Sugar	
2 Cans Milk	25
Butter 1lb	45
Gasoline	50
	3.00
By Fish - 16 lbs @ 10¢	1.60
Cash	1.40
	$3.00

Expenses for Trip

Engine	60 00
Attachm't	5 50
Spark plugs	1 25
Oil (1 gal.)	1 00
Hooks	1 10
Line	1 60
Express charges	1 00
4 Batteries	2 00
Razor Sharpener	25
R. Stamp	50
Stamps	10
Cup	1 00
Hooks	1 23
2 Films	90
Pictures (Falk)	2 36
Mitts (3 pairs)	50
Overalls 2 pr @ 125	2 50
Socks	1 00
Fix	85
Teeth Extraction	1 75
Hr Cut	60
Razor Sharpend	35

Elling G. Seglem

1923

Memoranda

E.A. SEGLEM
Fisherman's Home
ISLE ROYALE

Thursday June 7th

After much meditating I packed my duds—unpacked them and repacked them several times. John* took me down to the depot in his lizzie. Ma and Mamie* went along. Took the North American* N.W. at 10 o'clock. The trip uneventful. Steam was turned on and I put my feet on the pipes and felt very comfortable. No sleep. Had lunch at 7:30 at Eau Claire, Wisc.

Friday June 8th.

(On the train) The sun came out nice and warm and made it pleasant. Enjoyed the beautiful scenery around Eau Claire and Chippewa Falls—beautiful indeed. Landed at 1:30 in Duluth and had lunch—baked trout. Weather nice and warm. Went up to E.T.'s and found them home. Ordered provisions and called on Tronvick.* Had a good night's sleep and felt fine.

Saturday June 9

Loafed around all day in the city. Brought my baggage to the str. dock and bought passage for the island. Went out to the lighthouse and took a couple of snapshots. Also went over on Minnesota Point* and had lunch. Met a fellow from St. Paul—very agreeable person. Went over to Tronvick's in the evening and from there to E.T.—had ice cream and cake. Hit the hay about 10 and had a good night's sleep. Weather ideal.

Sunday June 10

Left Duluth for the Isle on the Str. "America." The weather was beautiful, calm and warm. Reached Grand Marais about dusk—took a short walk while the freight was unloaded and then hit the bunk.

Monday June 11th

Got up about 4:30 and went out on deck to find boat passing Pigeon River—the boundary between U.S. and John Bull. The weather was ideal and the scenery along the coast undescribably beautiful. Got into Ft. William about 7 o'clock and Port Arthur about 8:30. Left P.A. at 9 o'clock and reached Isle Royale 12:^{00}—Fisherman Home at 6:^{00}.

Tuesday June 12th

Fixed up my belongings and surveyed the stuff left here 2 yrs ago. Found all in good shape except one oar missing and my little oil stove rusted and useless. Had fish dinner at E.T. Took a stroll with Halloran's boat down to the point but nothing doing. Boat leaking pretty badly but will tighten up in day or two.

Wednesday June 13th

Woke up during the night as the wolves were barking around the cabin. Got up early and rigged up the sail and tried it out and the good old ship"ALMIDA" sails along as proudly as a full rigger. Out trolling caught 1 fish. Storm started—wind blew strong—rain and thunder at night.

Thursday June 14

Strong N.E. and heavy sea. —kind of chilly. Wrote several letters and post cards. Went out to the steamer. Went out trolling , not a bite. That fandangle muskerino don't get them.

Friday June 15

Windy day. Went out to the point and caught 4.

Saturday June 16

Out trolling—caught 3.

Sunday June 17th

Rolled out of my comfortable bunk after a good night's sleep and made flopjacks and coffee. Put away a whole dozen—oh boy! Went out to the point with E.T.'s hired man and into Siskiwit Bay caught 4—then home for dinner—then back to the bay again and caught 8 beauties. My hands and _____ very sore from rowing.

June 18

The wind was blowing from SW and lake choppy. Went over the breakers at 11 a.m. and into the bay—caught 7 trout. Prepared 27 fish for shipment but the lousy str didn't stop—the pesky Ginks.

June 19

Out trolling in the Bay but a storm was forming and I hiked for home. Got home just before the hurry cane. Got 4 trout.

June 20

Stormy day—foggy and chilly. Wrote letter to Esther. Took it easy all day.

June 21st

A stiff breeze from the NE to E blowing, with fog and choppy sea. The fish spoiled so all I can do is to hang crepe on my nose. Hope to get mail today. Sent 2 films to Graber. Letters from Esther, Alice, Ma, Storey, Lawrence, and return from Theodore—Letters and cards from 18th. Sent also one to Esther.

June 22

Rained like sixty nearly all night. A warm foggy morning. Took a row down to Boat Harbor in the a.m. Had fish dinner at E.T. Went sailing on the bay in my good old ship "Almida." Wind blowing from East.

June 23rd

A bum day. Tried to do a little trolling—only 1 fish.

Sunday June 24

Got up about 7. Made flopjacks—had a big breakfast and went out trolling. Caught 8 in the forenoon in the Bay. Sailed from F.H. to Siskiwit point. Olaf came down in the Gas boat and towed me home. Had dinner and went out again. The gas boat towed my skiff and Halloran's boat into the bay and we trolled in a squally sea and strong wind. Caught 8 more. Storm forming so we gassed home.

June 25th

Went out trolling in the morning and caught 13. Wind getting strong. Edw. towed me home from S. point. Mrs. S., the kids and chicken arrived. Moved into Olaf's house. Big Bull Moose on the beach. Shipped 88 lbs. — 28 fish. Got letters from Edith, Ma, Koch, and Hagstad—also newspapers.

June 26th

Got up about 7 and made breakfast. Wind blowing strong from S.W. and weather doubtful. Went out to the point but wind blowing whites in the bay so went home and had dinner at E.T.'s. Went out in P.M. and caught 5. Made flopjacks for supper.

Mrs. S. (E.T.s wife) on left with Almida at a later date

June 27th

A threatening morning went out to Sisk Point and caught 2 nice trout, one 8 lb. and one 6 lbs. The wind changed to N. and I went out to the Rocks and caught 4 small ones. Back home for lunch and sailed down to S. point again and caught 1. E.T. towed me home.

June 28

A windy blustry day. Went out to Siskiwit Point in a strong wind and choppy sea. Edw towed me out—caught one trout but wind increased and "Norlands Jachter."* Sailed for Seglem's Harbor.

June 29

Up at 5:30—made breakfast and went out fishing to Siskiwit Point. Caught 11 trout—among them 4 big boys. Got back for dinner at E.T. Had Kompa. A squaly hot day. Felt a little tired at night.

June 30th

Windy, blustry day. Caught only 1 trout.

July 1st

Went to Hay Bay to call on Lively and Bjorvek and Kvalvick.* Had a duce of a time with Olaf. Rained "pitchforks." Got home 8 p.m. Cold and tired.

Ed Kvalvick

July 2nd

Went out to the point trolling in the forenoon—caught 4 trout. Got back home at 1 o'clock and made dinner then. Cleaned my fish for the boat. The gas boat rammed the America and shoved the oars through the sides of the boat and broke both oars. Got back in a sinking condition. Shipped 16 fish.

July 3rd.

Slept about 11 hours last night. Got up at 7:30 and made breakfast and went out to Redfin. Hooked up a 30 and a 16 pounder and two smaller ones. Got hungry and rowed home and cooked dinner—then went back to Redfin and caught 4 more in the P.M. Rowed about 12 miles.

July 4
Had a good night's sleep. Got up at 5:30. E.T. towed me to the reef of the Rocks. Went back and forth once and caught 5 small ones. Rowed to S.P. and the Bay—caught 1—cooked coffee in the bay and had lunch. Got home at noon. Took a lay down til 1:30. Went to Redfin and caught 4. Home at 6. Made supper and felt a little bit tired after rowing about 14 miles. Oh Hum!

July 5th
Wind blowing from NE and increasing—kicking up quite a rough sea. Very foggy in A.M.

July 6th
A very bummy day. Chilly, foggy—and windy with a downpour of rain. Kept indoor with fire in the stove all day. Had a nice dinner of Skolt* and spuds—coffee and bread and the good stuff.

July 7th
Another bad day. Nothing doing on the lake—was out and tried it out but got only one bite. The weather being rotten.

July 8 Sunday
More bummy weather. Caught one poor feesh at Redfin.

July 9 Monday
Ditto ditto—with fog and rain. Had no shipment. Boat very late. Letters from Abe and Clarence.

July 10 Tuesday
Windy, but otherwise a fair day. Wind going down about noon. Went out to Redfin and the point. Caught 3 fish. Fried one for supper and eat half of it with hot spuds and coffee.

July 11
Lake calm early in the morning. Went to the rocks and caught 3. Wind increasing—rowed home and fixed up my belongings prep to leaving.

June	Fish Caught		
13	Reef	1	
15	Sincoust Pt.	4	5
16	" "	3	8
17	" Bay	12	20
18	" "	7	27
19	" "	4	31
23	" "	1	32
24	" "	16	48
25	" "	13	61
26	" Paul	5	66
27	Sinc Pt & Rocks	7	73
28	"	1	74
29		11	85
30	"	2	87
July 2		4	91
" 3	Redfin 7. S.P. 1	8	99
	& 16 lbs.		
4	Rocks S.P. & Redfin	9	108
9		2	110
10	"	3	113

225 ft. Fish line	$1.35
1 Dodger	1.10
1 Cap	1.45
1 Skinner Hook	50
Memo Book	10
Mos. Netting	90
G's Insurance	45
Pictures	45
Crfr	25
XX	1 50
K.O.T.M. #5	8 05
mitts	15
~~thermometer~~	
(Films) 4	1 80
Stamps	1 00
H.W. Bag ✓	
Rubber bands ✓	
Sail ✓ (Lllgls)	
Trout fly ✓	15
" HKs	15

1924

MEMO

ISLE ROYALE

TRIP

1924 Diary of Elling A. Seglem

Tuesday June 3d

Kalsomined the front ceiling and started to get things in shape for my trip.

Got my "traps" together and packed up my belongings ready for the trip.

June 3 Tue

Kalsomined* the front ceiling and started to get things in shape for my trip. Got my "traps"* together and packed up my belongings ready for the trip.

June 4 Wed

All aboard for Minneapolis. Took the 10:35 Burlington and had a very fine trip along the beautiful Mississippi River. Arrived in Minneapolis about 11:30 p.m. Met at the depot by Herman and his family who took me home to their house and made me feel comfortable.

June 5th

Herman had his flivver ready and we drove around nearly all day sightseeing. Visiting Halloran, and found him not home. Went to the lakes and Ft. Snelling, the new Ford Plant in St. Paul. Hunted up Mr. & Mrs. McLeod. Herman and I went riding right after breakfast and were out nearly all day sightseeing. Had supper at Mr. Wold's. Miss Wold had been playing ball and got bumped in the eye. She got a dandy black "shunty." Will leave for Duluth at 11:20 tonight on the Great Northern R.R.

June 7 Sat

Arrived at Duluth at 6:30 this morning. Did not sleep a wink all night. Funny, isn't it? Some people can snore on a RR train. One gink made more noise than the train. Had breakfast. Went to Fred Erickson and ordered my provision, then over to E.T.'s. He don't look very strong. Begged me to stay over 'til Wed and he would go along. I reluctantly consented.

E.T. and Elling

June 8 Sun

A chilly **dreary** day. Took my camera and went down to the lighthouse and went to John Skadberg for dinner, together with Mr. & Mrs. E.T. and Magda. John Skadberg took us over to Pete in the p.m. Had supper at Pete's. John took us home in his auto in a cold rain. Caught a slight cold and felt kind of choked up during the night. Wish I had gone with the steamer this morning although the lake was rough and threatening. Took snapshot of Ski Jump and dog

June 9 Mon

Went out shopping in the morning. Had dinner down town. Baked lake trout and I surely enjoyed it. Took in a show in the afternoon to pass the time away. Duluth is certainly some dreary city. Am glad I don't live here.

June 10 Tue

Took a ride with Thorvald to the East End and then down to the lake. Met a couple from Nebraska. Had my picture taken by them on the rocky shore. Met Mr. Bergersen. Met Gertie downtown, also John. Went to Tronvick's for supper. Got back to E.T. at 10 pm. Glad tomorrow is Boatday so I can make a get away from this cheesy burg.

June 11 Wed

I am glad to get away from this bloomin' town. The good old tub "America" cast loose at 10 a.m. and off I am for the dear old fish hole. Very few passengers on the boat. Passed Standard Rock at 3 p.m. Mrs. Williams stood on the cliff waving a big white sheet. I was up on the upper deck with my field glass and could see her plainly. Arr at Grand Marais before sundown. Fine day on the lake.

June 12 Thurs

Arrived at Ft. William at 5 a.m. and at Port Arthur at 6:30. Had breakfast and took a stroll up town. Some "sleepy hollow" Pt. Arthur! Nothing stirring. Took picture of dog and cannons. Left 8 a.m. for I.R. Arrived at Belle Isle at 11 a.m. and at Siskiwit Bay 4:30. Met the boys out in the bay and Ingvald Seglem, cousin, took me over to Fisherman's Home in his gas boat. Arrived F.H. 5:30. Got my stuff ready for bed. Had a light supper. Got a tremendous greeting by the wolves—they must be glad I came.

June 13th Friday

After a thrilling night of howling racket caused by a pack of wolves near the cabin I got up about 7 o'clock and made breakfast after which I got my things in shape. Boat in bad shape. Stern all rotten. Worked on the boat nearly all day. Got it in fairly good shape and its now ready for the paint brush. The weather is fine. Sunshine and calm and warm. Moved into the "Hotel" and fixed me up a fine bunk and although alone I feel fine and contented.

June 14th Sat

Well, the wolves surely did their best to entertain me last night again and so did also a frog. It's some music, but I like it. Tried out the trolling and got a dandy Kogefisk. Got back at noon and Oh Boy! did I prepare a swell dinner. Eat half the fish and will have the other half tomorrow. Painted the good old craft "ALMIDA" and she looks slick. Repaired the roof of my cabin. Weather fine but now it looks like rain—well let it. I got my roof fixed so it won't leak on me.

June 15 Sun

The weather is simply fine but it's kind of windy. So I can't go out this morning. Wish I had a shot gun so I could have duck soup for dinner. Well, the wind is "going down" so I will try it out. Not so bad—went out along the reef towards Redfin Island and Oh Boy! Caught 6 speckled beauties—two

8 pounders. That's pretty good for a start. I'll say. Will have some for the boat tomorrow anyhow. Hope E.T. comes.

June 16th Mon

Well today is boat day and I hope to hear from home. Some strange fine big ducks paid me a visit. Went out to the steamer expecting to take off E.T. but he was not on the boat—must have had a bad attack of rheumatism. Made my first shipment—6 trout about 24 lbs. That's a pretty good start. Weather is surely fine.

June 17th Tue

Another fine day. Rowed over to Boat Harbor and caught a trout on the way. Took a trip across Siskiwit Bay to get the mail the steamer left there. Lake as calm as a mirror. Took me only 50 minutes to cross the bay—3 miles. That's going some. Had coffee at Ingvald's in Hay bay—they surely occupy a rough looking shack. Received letter & cards from Esther—Union card from Hardiland and Visergutten.*

June 18, 1924

Slept till 8 o'clock this morning. A strong S.E. is blowing and the lake is very rough. Glad I came back last night. Wrote letters to E.T. & Esther, cards to Otto, Baude, Alex, McLeod, Abe, Morbro, Walstrom, Koch. It looks pretty ugly and I am in for a stormy night. The wind is blowing and lake is roaring. I am afraid the boat won't pass tomorrow.

June 19th

It poured down all night with thunder & lightning and the gale is still blowing from the east and the sea is roaring like a lion. Got out of bed at 9:15 to find my pants soaked from drippings through the roof. Good thing I repaired the roof or I would have been drowned out. No chance for the steamer to stop here today. It would be suicide to try and get out through the surf. Never saw the lake so ugly. It's been raining all day and it looks tough. Hope E.T. isn't on the boat as he can't land here today. Great storm all day.

June 20th Friday

"Thar she Blows!" The steamer is blowing for me? 6 a.m. and all is well. Get out of bed and see. The storm is abating and the steamer is off my place. A strong wind is blowing from the SW. Didn't go out and steamer proceeded on its way. Anderson & Olson* came in from Rock Harbor, bound for Long

Point. Windbound they put up in Olaf's shack for the day. Got a dozen eggs from them and they "saved the day." Fixed up a screen door and now I am safe from skeeters.

John Skadberg and
Sivert Anderson in "Bess"

June 21 Sat

The boys departed at 4 a.m. for Long Point. Windy blustry day. Couldn't get out to do any fishing.

June 22 Sun

The wind blew a gale all morning but calmed down a little in the afternoon. Went out trolling and caught seven. Storm cloud forming and I went home. Big storm bursted at about 9 o'clock—rain, thunder & lightning. The wolves were howling again. The lightning, thunder, and rain was something "terrific."

June 23 Mon

Got out of bed at 5 o'clock and went out fishing and was back at 10. Rowed out to the reefs and point and the bay. Caught 6 trout. Went out to steamer in a strong west wind and heavy sea and delivered the fish and got mail from Ma, Halloran, Ingvald, and Mrs. E.T. also Visergutten. Accidently didn't get the mail sent. When I reached shore I found I had not delivered the mail. The bag was mixed up in the covering I had over the fish box.

June 24 Tue

This has been a lazy day for me. I've been lying down reading and taking it easy nearly all day. A strong chilly sou'wester has been blowing all day. Expected the boys from Rock Harbor to come by from Long Point but the lake is probably too rough for them. 4 o'clock and here they come! Left 4:30 for Wright's Island.* Arr. W.I. 6 Left R.I.* 6:30 Arr. Rock Harbor 9:30. Met Bill Lively & company at R.I.

June 25 Wed

Had a good night's sleep at Anderson's house. Stept into Johnsons & Olson's camp and had coffee and flapjacks. Went greenstone picking and over to Mike Johnson's* for eggs and bread. After dinner I went Greenstone

Rock Harbor Lighthouse

hunting, found a few small ones. Took picture of old Light house.* Went over on Cemetery Island* and investigated the old graves. Took a row around in Anderson's skiff. Took picture of graves.

June 26 Thurs
Bought wolf fur. Took pictures of Anderson and his wolf pelts. Had fish dinner at Anderson's. Got on the America for Fisherman's Home but hadn't gone there so had to get off at Hay Bay at Ingvald's. Slept at Ingvald's shack and with Mr. Rude* and George

Graves on Cemetery Island

were going to to F.H. but the Ginks didn't come in time so the trip was postponed. Got letter from Roy saying he and Laverne are coming Monday.

June 27 Fri
Had a short night's sleep. Got up at 3:30 and went out. Went back to bed again and laid around till 5:30. Rude and Geo. came over in the skiff and we rowed over to Fisherman's Home. Went trolling but 000. Roald Skelbred and two other Oibu's came from Washington Harbor. Olga Seglem was with. Had lunch at E.T. shack, then came over to Seglem's Cabin and we had lemonade. George and his dad put up their tent and made camp. Weather threatening and wolves are howling.

June 28 Sat
Another windy day and no good for fishing. Made a landing net for the boys and took it easy pretty nearly the whole day. Went out a few hours toward night but caught only two trout. The weather settled down to a dead calm toward evening. The wolves scared George and his dad out of the tent late at night and they came running over to my cabin and stayed here all night.

June 29 Sun
Got up at 5 o'clock and went out on the lake as the weather was fine. Rowed out to the channel, over to the point, back to the reefs and out to

the rocks and back just in time to dodge a big rain squall which bursted at noon. Got just one little nibble.

June 30 Mon

Well, the America is now coming through the channel and I'll have to get out and take off Roy and Laverne. There is E.T. on the boat also with a big load of stuff. The skiff is pretty well loaded down. Wonder if it will carry it all without tipping. Better sit still. She's on the pivot of balance. The boys are bringing all kinds of good stuff from home. Oh Joy!

July 1st Tue

Well, the boys are getting ready for action and preparing for strenuous work. Went out trolling and the first one caught was a 10 pounder.

July 2nd Wed

The boys were out trolling and caught quite a few. I made them a raft and they had a great time on the bay. Roy shot a rabbit and went swimming. They seem to like this place. The weather is fine and warm.

July 3rd 1924 Thurs

Got the boys out of bed at 5 a.m. Had a substantial breakfast and went on the lake at 6. Went out to Redfin Island and was back at 10. Fishing no good—caught only 2 fish—a 13 pounder and one smaller, boys caught 2 in afternoon. Shipped 66 pounds—16 fish. Got pictures from Herman. Rude got his boat off the America. The wolves gave the boys a concert in the evening.

July 5th Saturday

It rained quite a bit last night and I let the boys sleep as long as they wanted as the wind is blowing strong from S.W. and we can't get out. They got in about 12 hrs sleep. Boys went out in the P.M. and caught a few trout in the bay.

July 6th Sun

Made 18 flapjacks for breakfast. The boys and I took a trip out to the rocks and McCormick's reefs. An ideal day—calm and sunshine all day. Caught 15 trout—one weighing 31 1/2 lbs and one 20—one 15, and the boys are tick-led "pink" with the great sport. Took lunch along and had dinner or lunch on the Attwood Beach. Got back home at 8 o'clock well satisfied at being on the "go" all day. I rowed about 20 miles but felt "bully" just the same.

July 7th Mon

The boys slept till 8:30. I went out on the lake and got back just as they had rolled out. Roy and I went out to the Rocks and got two—one 20 pounds and one 11. Got back about 1 o'clock. Cleaned 35 trout for the boat. Had a dandy shipment of 190 pounds. Received bread and eggs from Rock Harbor and pictures from Minneapolis.

July 8 Tue

A bummy day. Boys went out to Redfin and caught 2 small trout. I went out there too and caught 2. Got caught in a dense fog going home and by a slick piece of navigation hit the gap after rowing around in the fog a long time without seeing a trace of land. The fog continued all day and we didn't attempt to go out again.

July 9 Wed

A blustery windy day, and although nice on shore we could not get out to do any fishing. Just hung around our cabin and confined our gloom within our hearts. But the boys are cheerful and apparently contented and happy.

July 10 Thurs

Another windy, stormy, and foggy day and we had quite a time getting out to the steamer. Otto Gronbeck* came off the boat and was introduced to his "doubtful" new home. He brought with him a half ham and some goat cheese which came in "mity" good as we didn't recieve the provisions we had ordered and expected to get when the boat came.

July11 th Friday

Another bum day. Will the weather ever behave itself? This is getting on a fellow's nerves. Weather bad and no fish! Can you beat it? Will pull up stakes if it keeps on and go to Washington Harbor.

July 12 Sat

Excursion to Siskiwit Bay. Roy, LaVerne, Otto and I went into the very bottom of the bay, 7 miles from Francis Point.* Visited Halloran's Landing and the old mining cabins at "Camp Cepeck 714." Caught 5 nice ones and got caught in a big squall. Had to take shelter in the old Powder House where we huddled into one corner of the roofless ruin of 70 odd bygone years until the storm blew over. Caught 3 trout.

July 13th Sun

Just a year ago today I left for home (1923). This morning the boys and I went to McCormick's reefs. But the wind increased so we couldn't do much trolling. Had lunch on the beach and on the homeward stretch went back on the reefs and caught 2 trout. Wind changed to a S.W. gale and we coasted all the way back on the white caps. Otto prepared "Mulligan" for supper.

July 14 Monday

Another very blustery day. Gale blowing from sou'west and we had a awful task getting out to the steamer. Mrs. E.T. came. Otto, Roy, and I went out in the skiff and got our grocery order. Otto bought meat, bread, 2 pies and chocolate, and we had a great feast after we got home. Otto is quite a Mulligan Cook. Got letter from home and newspaper from New York and "Visergutten." Had mulligan's pot roast for supper.

July 15th Tue

A beautiful day on the shore but no good on the lake. Strong S.W. blowing all day. LaV & Otto went into the bay in the p.m., came back with 6. One a 11 lb. Roy and Dad went out in the morning but got 000. Laid around and fattened our hides all afternoon.

July 16th Wed

Mr. Rude came over and said:"Do you want a joy ride?" and of course we said, "Yes." He towed us (two boats—the "Almida" and the "Shamrock") to McCormick's reefs. Roy and LaVerne caught 3 fish, a 25, 17 and 11 pounders. Otto and I caught 3—42 1/2,15 and 13. The 42 1/2 lbs. boy is a record breaker. Had a very exciting time getting that boy into the boat.

July 17th Thurs

This is boat day again. Went to the reef alone and caught two small trout. Had pictures taken of the big fish—42 1/2 pounder. Shipped the big fellow with head on. Shipped 8 fish—92 lbs.

July 18th Fri

Otto, Roy, LaVerne & I went to McCormick's but Roy and LaVerne only went half way. Otto and I caught two big fish and 3 smaller ones and the boys caught 3. Passed Olson from Rock Harbor at the rocks. He came back late in the evening and put in here for the night. Boys decided to go with him in the morning to RH to pick green stones.

July 19th Sat
The boys went to RH with Olson, Otto left F.H. I went to McCormick and caught 2 big fish.

July 20 Sun
A windy blustry day on the lake but fine on shore. Bill Lively and his wife came over from Hay. Took picture of the crowd in front of Rude's Camp.

July 21 Mon
Another bad day with a big downpour of rain and thick fog. Steamer about 3 hours late. Boys came back from Rock Harbor. Got letter from John and Olga and Mrs. W. also candy and films and papers and magazines from Esther. Mrs. S. baked a big dandy cake for us.

July 22nd Tue
Another windy day; decided to move to W.H. and started to pack up ready to leave as soon as the weather gets nice.

July 23 Wed
The morning early was calm but rain started and when it stopped we put our stuff in the skiff and prepared to go to W.H. The bunch from W.H. came to Fisherman's Home. The boys and I said farewell and rowed to McCormicks' where the W.H. bunch picked us up and towed us to W.H. Where we found a snug house and prepared to stop there henceforth. Arrived there about 6:30 p.m., cold, hungry and a little wet from rain. Caught one fish at McCormick's.

July 24 Thurs
Went out trolling a little and caught 4 little fellows. Some difference between these skimps and the whoppers we are used to be catching at F.H. and McCormick's. America came with our trunk, suitcases and a lot of mail and a box of cookies for LaV. Everybody happy and the girls came over for the

Fish house at Washington Harbor

boys and Roy went with them to a dance.

July 25 Fri
Went out trolling a little and caught 7 little trout. Rowed around the islands—Johnson Island and Thompson Island*—also in through the bays and all around.

July 26 Sat
A very foggy day and no good for trolling or getting out on the lake so we just laid around the shore and took it easy until in the afternoon. We went out and caught 7 small ones.

July 27 &28 Sun & Mon
Nothing doing. Sunday didn't go out at all. —Monday we caught 2 little fish. Oh hum! Washington Harbor is a punk place for trolling.

July 29 Tue
Took a trip to club house in Nels's boat.

30 Wed
Caught 5 fish.

31 Thurs
LaVerne went home.

August 1st Fri
Towed to lower point Rainbow Cove. Trolled all the way back, got 2 trout.

2 Sat
An awful windy day. Visited Sivertsen* and Martinson. Concert at Nels' in evening. Big storm during the night

3 Sun
Went with Nels, Olga, Ole and Roy to Lake Feldman. Met Martinson on the beach coming back.

4th Mon
The bunch came from Grand Marais with their instruments on the America. Big reception on the dock. Big dance at the hall.

5th Tue
4 boats—40 people went to the club house on an excursion concert on the Rocks and dance in our house.

6thWed
Went trolling and caught 8 trout. Over to Martinson for lunch and Jollification in afternoon. Dance at hall in evening.

7th Thur
Left Washington Harbor.

8th Fri
Arrived at Standard Rock.

United States and Dominion Transportation Co.

Steamer Schedules

TWO TRIPS WEEKLY
IN EACH DIRECTION
between
DULUTH,
FT. WILLIAM - PT. ARTHUR
ISLE ROYALE PORTS
and NORTH SHORE PORTS

SOUTH SHORE
ONE TRIP WEEKLY
IN EACH DIRECTION
between
DULUTH, PORT WING, HERBSTER
and CORNUCOPIA

Passenger and Freight Line
For full information apply to
L. P. HOGSTAD —or— W. D. EMIL
Supt. DULUTH, MINN. Traffic Manager, CHICAGO, ILL.

EXPENDITURES				Preliminaries and on the Journey			
						50	04
6 Films @ 45c	2	70		Picture (minnehaha)			50
Mosquito Netting		25		Bar & bag			46
Paint	1	10	X	Due		8	11
Glass		4		Provision - Erickson	20	00	
Fare to Minnpls	14	66		Address Book			25
" " Duluth	5	40	X	Pts		8	00
" " Isle Royale	19	80		Hook			50
Storage	1	24		Line		1	75
Lunch		30	X	Flash Light			60
"		30	X	Field Glass	15	00	
"		25		Pens			5
"		10		Not Book (this)			35
"	1	50		Medicine (all my order)			40
"		40		Mosquit dope			45
"		20		Caller			20
Stamps	1	00		Tip			25
Snapshot (Kot)		10		Post Cards Duluth			18
Post Cards (Minn)		25		" " Tobin			10
Ice Cream		50				107	21

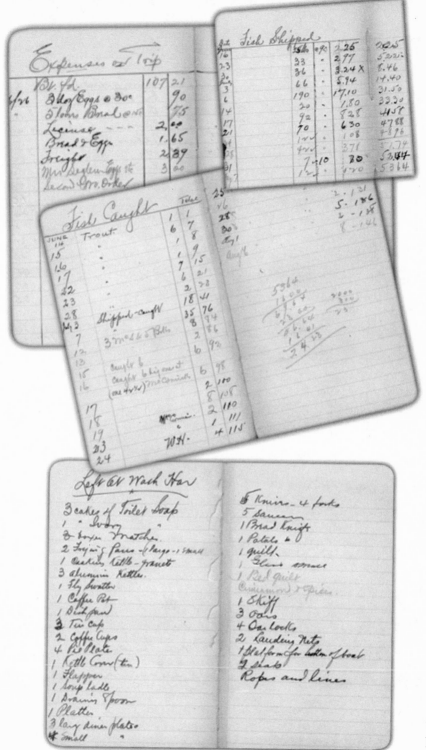

113

1932

Student's

SERIES

Junior Note Book

No. 782

Name *E.A. Seglem*

Grade *4514 N. Troy Street*

Isle Royale Trip

1932

A Record

of the

Isle Royale Trip

— " —

Summer of 1932

by

Elling G. Seglem

starting from
Chicago

Thursday June 2nd at

5:25 St time 5 o'clock A.M.

in company with

Roy and Eleanor

Thursday, June 2d

Left Chicago at 5:35 S.T. —Raise Cary 6:50; Woodstock 7:20, Harvard* 7:40; Walworth 7:55; Darien 8:07; Whitewater 8:40; Ft. Atkinson 9:00; Lake Ripley 9:20; Madison 10; Left Mad. 10:35; Stopped for lunch 11:45; Sauk City 12:05; Mill Bluff (Took Picture) 12:30; Gotham (Roy's Pipe on the Bum) 1:22; Sextonville 1:38; Richland Center 1:45 (ice cream); Stopped at spring and had a refreshing drink 2:18; Readstown 3:00; arr. Viroqua* at Johnson's Place 4:45; stayed there over Night and left 5:45 am Friday for Duluth.

This was one ideal day of sightseeing thru the most wonderful scenery from Madison. Mrs. Johnson and the Johnson family were glad to see us and certainly treated us royally.

The Newlyweds* felt happy and enjoyed the first day of their Honeymoon trip immensely.

Friday June 3rd

Got up early (4:30) and Mrs. Johnson made a big breakfast for us and at 5:45 A.M. we were off on our Second leg of our journey. La Crosse* 7:00; Winona 8:00; Lake City 9:40; Red Wing 10:00; Hastings, 11:45 (had dinner); left 12:20 St Paul 1:25; Duluth* 6:30. Ran into fierce rainstorm between St. P. & Duluth. Stopped at Tronvik and Seglems.* They were glad to see us.

Roy and Eleanora

This ended the 2nd day of our Journey. A very charming trip thru the wonderful scenery of Coon Valley and along the beautiful Mississippi River from La Cross to St. Paul. The weather was fine and helped to make this day's trip very much enjoyable to all of us. Went over to Pete Skadberg's in evening. Weather chilly & foggy.

Saturday June, 4th

Went with Roy and Eleanora down to the dock and made arrangements for passage from G.M.* Ordered our groceries and had a big fish dinner after a ride over the ridge boulevard. Went in to Kelly's and took a slant at the prize fish. They have moved it to the front of the store now so it is in a very conspicuous place.

Duluth seems dead as far as big business is concerned. Very seldom a steamboat Siren could be heard, and everybody complaining of hard times. I slept with E.T. The Newlyweds put up at Mr. Tronvik's cozy home.

Sunday June 5th

Got up about 8 o'clock and had breakfast at E.T.s. Felt peculiar as my stomach was not working right, and had somewhat of a scare as to conditions. Went down to drugstore and bought a fountain syringe and took a douche at Tronvik's. Then to E.T.'s for dinner. Left about 2 o'clock for the North Shore. Fog. Stopped at Knife River a few moments and said hello to Hansens and Hans Mindestrom. Then on to Gooseberry River where we stopped and took pictures. Then on to Beaver Bay to William's where we were received with open arms and eats galore. Stomach on the bum again(?)

Monday June 6th

Had a fairly good night's sleep alongside of old William although he was snoring and blowing right into my ear. Weather foggy and a little chilly, and not very encouraging for a lake trip. Took a walk with Roy and El over to Thorvald and met Lauritz Larson who is building a home there. In the evening Mrs. Midbrod and Mrs. Whiting came over and we had a long chat. Old W. told some queer tales which made everybody scream.

Stomach very much on the bum and I became somewhat alarmed at my condition. Black flies and Mosquitoes were very troublesome.

Tuesday June 7th

Left William's place about 10^{15}. Telephoned to Duluth if Winyah* had left. A gale blowing from Northeast and the sea running high. Fog had cleared and a sunshiny day. Arrived at Grand Marais about 1 o'clock. Met Charlie Seglem and stayed there until boat time. Boat didn't come till 3 o'clock in the morning (Wednesday) owing to storm—7 hrs late. Stayed in Coast Guard Station and had a 3 hr. nap there before the boat came.

Johnny Nelson conveyed our baggage to the dock. Chas. S. went with us to the dock and left us about 10 o'clock. Storm abating now.

Wednesday June 8th

3:00 A.M. The Winyah blew for Grand Marais and we all jumped into our duds and scrambled over to the dock where we put aboard our baggage and our sleepy eyed carcasses and off we went.

I forgot to mention that I went to see the Dr. yesterday and got some "torpedoes" for my bum stomach. and now I am feeling O.K. ($2.00)

The weather was excellent and we spent a pleasant day on the lake, reached Isle Royale about 11$\underline{^{00}}$ and at about 5 were taken off by John S. and taken over to Seglem's Harbor in his boat. He gave us 2 dandy trout for dinner and we made 3 meals out of them. Reached Seglem's Harbor about 6$\underline{^{30}}$. The boys stayed for supper.

Thursday June 9th

Had a good night's sleep and a good breakfast. Then got the boat out the Ice house and painted her up with green trim. She looks good and is in fine condition. Also overhauled the "Shamrock." Rude came last night. Got all our stuff fixed up and now the only thing to wait for is the paint to dry on the boat and out we will go.

The weather is excellent—warm Sunshine and the lake calm. and everything looks good here. So come what may—we're now settled down for a few weeks.

John Skadberg and his partner came over in his boat in the P.M.

Friday June 10th

Got up early and as I came over to the fish house a cow moose stood in the bay near the fish house. I called Roy and Eleanora and when they came she swam across the bay. Roy and I put up the flag pole and were nearly eaten alive by black flies and mosquitoes. Then we dug out the old flag and hoisted it and it sure looks good.

Boy, oh Boy! Those Black devils did some damage to my neck. It's swollen up like the Rocky Mountains. The weather remains fine and warm, and the coyutes are entertaining us with their music.

Saturday June 11th

Put the boats in the water, and got our fishing tackle in shape. Got the motor ready and tried her out. She works pretty good and seems to send the boat along at a faster speed. We took a trip around the Seg's Island with Eleanora. She was a little timid and scared at first but after she got initiated calmed down

Seglem Cabin with flagpole

and I think she will soon like the boat. Mrs. Rude is out with him early and late. This morning they were over at 3:30 to lift their nets.

Sunday June 12th

The Winyah came along about 2 o'clock and we went over and took Eric* off the boat. He came along with a big smile on his fizz and after he got established Roy and I took him for a ride across Siskiwit bay to see our friends Ed Kvalvik and Mr. Bjorvek. They were glad to see us. Stayed there a little while. Then back for supper. It was a beautiful day, the lake calm and a warm sun made things beautiful and pleasant. Eric is somewhat struck with the beauty of Seg's Harbor. Got my Barometer and pennant pole and letter from Esther.

Monday June 13th

Took a trip into the Brooktrout stream and caught 3 dandy speckled beauties which we fried on the beach at Siskiwit River,* and had a dandy meal.

The wind (N.E.) kicked up a choppy surf and when we landed at Siskiwit River our propeller struck a rock and put it on the blink, but Roy fixed so we got home with it o. k. On the way home we trolled and got 5 trout. Eleanora was a little frightened but as the lake calmed down she got OK again. Eric and the rest enjoyed the trip up through the river for about a mile. Some beauty spot. Took several pictures. Sam and John came with their rig.

Tuesday June 14th

Went out to Redfin Island in the P.M. with Roy and Eric but the SW was blowing strong and the lake choppy so we beat it for Siskiwit Bay where we caught 4 trout. Eric had a dandy big one up to the boat but fumbled and the whopper got away from us.

The game warden came along and fixed Roy up with license so now he is happy.

Eric seems to enjoy his trip immensely, and is getting pretty well burnt up. He has a dandy red beak and a good sized appetite. He caught 3 of the fish and is elated over his fishing prowess. Heard the whippoorwills singing for first time

Wednesday June 15th

Went out to Winyah with Rude and shipped 23 lbs. Got letter from Ma & Alice. Made ready to take trip to McCormick's. Got there at 2:30 and put Roy and Eleanora in Halloran's boat, Eric and I in my boat. Eric hooked up a 4 pounder and a 22 lb baby was my first catch. Then a 10 pounder and a 15 pounder Trolled around 'til 6 o'clock. Roy and Eleanora didn't get a bit. Then for home and a big fish feast. El had baked some swell bread and you bet it was fine. Eric got quite a thrill out of that 22 lb whopper. He is getting as brown as a Nut. The weather was calm but a little foggy.

Thursday June 16th

A gray chilly windy morning. Did not go out this morning. Eric slept until 9:30 and so did Roy and Eleanora. I was up at 7 but let them sleep. John Skadberg and Ronning* came in and had dinner with us after which we took a spin out to Redfin Island and trolled for a while without results.

Then we headed for Houghton Point and the Bay and caught 5 trout. Eric got two, Roy two, I one Four 3 lbs., one 5 lbs.—17 lbs. round, 14 dressed. The Skadbergs gave us some Menominees which we fried for supper and they were real good. Weather calm tonight with full moon illuminating the lake

Saw a wolf across the Bay

Friday June 17th

We got out of our bunk early and started for McCormick's. The wind was from N.E. blowing lightly and we had good going. When we reached the reefs it got a little rough so we headed for the beach where we tried out for Brookie, but nothing doing. So we explored inland about 1/2 Mile thru the brush. Found 4 Moose horns. Then to the beach for fried fish, tea, etc. Wind increasing and sea getting choppy. Waited till 4 P.M. for wind to go down, but no. Started for home at 4 in a choppy sea and headwind. Got home at 5:30. Sea getting rough and it looks like a bummy night ahead. Everybody happy and well fed.

Saturday June 18th

Started raining at 4 A.M. with a steady downpour 4 to 1 P.M.

Eric put away 12 flapjacks. He's red as a boiled lobster now. Fog rolling in with a W. Gale at 1 P.M. Roy baking "pocket books" in E.T.'s cabin, Eric writing, and so am I in my cabin. Rude gave us a nice Whitefish for supper. And you bet we had a swell feed from it—

Those "pocket books" and bran muffins Roy made were swell.

We trolled down at the point a little while toward evening and Eric got a 5 lb. and a 3 lb. – Roy and I got two 5 lbs. The air was somewhat chilly and a little heat in the Stove felt fine.

Sunday, June 19th

Got up about 6^{30} and went out alone to the point trolling. I did not want to wake the bunch but stole away quietly all by myself. Trolled till about 9 and got a 3 pounder and a 9 pound beauty. Got back and had breakfast. Wrote a letter to home, weighed my fish shipment which amounted to 75 lbs.

The Winyah came along about Noon and brought a package for Eric and letter from Esther.

Went over to the cave with the bunch, then took a nap in the afternoon while they went down to the point. Caught 6 (Eric 3, Roy 3) one a 14 lbs. 15 lbs. net. Took a little nap in the P.M.

Monday, June 20th

Started off for McCormick's –Roy, Eric and I—about 8:30 A.M. Trolled along the Rock reef on the way and hooked up 3 nice Trout 13, 9, 5. Then set off for McCormick in a Rain. Hooked up a 16 lbs., then a 5 lbs. The wind increased and we went ashore and had lunch—then tried out trolling again but nothing doing. Eric hooked up Isle Royale and thought he had a whopper, pulled so hard that the line broke and we had a hard time locating it—but we got it. Then hiked for home trolling the rock reefs again without a bite. Eric lost a big one. 34 lbs. Net.

Tuesday, June 21st

Roy came and roused us out of our snug bunk at 3:30. A beautiful sunrise 3:45. Eric took a picture of it.

Roy made flopjacks and after a big breakfast we started for the Rocks at 4:30. Eric caught a 4 pounder and a 5 lbs. and I caught a 11 lbs. Roy caught a 8 lbs. Then the lake got ruff and we headed for the Bay where we got 0. Then home for lunch.

Well, the weather is threatening so we did not go out again and now at 6 P.M. it's blowing hard and raining. Eric and I took a little nap in the P.M.

Wrote letter to A.E. Williamson and Anne Margrethe. Had fried trout for supper. Net fish 17 lbs.

Wednesday June 22nd

This is "Boat Day" and we have a shipment of 77 lbs. Got up at 3:30 and woke the crew. A beautiful Sunset and a fine morning. Roy made breakfast in a jiffy and out we went to the Rock reef and trolled till we were blue in the face without results. Then the wind blew up and we "hiked" for the bay. I got ashore at F.H. and the boys went. Then Roy hit for Redfin alone and caught a 6 lbs. Fine day in shore but a beast on the Lake. Went out with Rude to the Winyah in a heavy sea. After dinner I took a little nap, then Roy woke me and we took a strenuous hike up on the high ridge and down thru the swamp to Boat Harbor and back along the shore. Mosquitoes rambuncktious. Fried Herring for supper.

Thursday June 23d

A Windy Stormy day, chilly and bummy, although a fair day on shore, it was no day for fishing or outing.

The crew just laid around taking it easy. In the afternoon Eric went with Rude lifting nets and came back, after several hours on the lake, somewhat "frozen" but with a smile on his face.

Windy day at Seglem's Harbor

John Skadberg called in the afternoon and gave us 4 1/2 lbs. trout which we had for supper. Each one put away a trout, and by golly it sure was a dandy feast. Some appetite, I'll say!

Friday, June 24th

A most beautiful sunrise at 3:45 A.M. Took a snapshot of the wonderful sight. Then after a snappy lunch, set out for McCormick's alone. Motor got hot a little west of Boat Harbor, then for Rocks reef—Nothing doing; then home. A big Eagle parked on the fishhouse. Took pictures of it. Seemed tame, did not mind us walking around. Bingo! 8 ft. spr. Roy, El, and Eric went out trolling. They came back in a downpour of rain, cold and hungry with three fish. Eric had caught1 and Roy and El 2—9 pounds altogether. Had delicious fish cakes for supper.

Saturday, June 25th

A foggy morning—didn't go out on account of Roy fixing the Motor Coil.

Eric went out trolling alone in a strong S.W. Lost an oar and had a heck of time regaining it. He came back all tired out from rowing but without any fish.

Roy worked hard fixing the Motor and finally got her to kick off in good shape.

Brought the old stove over and made a hole in the wall to get it into the cabin. Now I am snugly ensconced in the "Hotel" with stove 'n' ev'ryt'ing.

Went down to the point and tried it out but nothing doing.

Sunday June 26th

Got out of our bunk at 4^{30} G.M. and went down to Redfin and Paul Islands and along the reefs. Roy and El caught a 5 lbs.

Then to the point and the bay. Nothing doing—Then Home.

Eric is packing up and is going to leave for good old Chicago on today's boat.

A calm foggy day and rain threatening.

Had flopjacks for lunch after we got back and how they disappeared.

Took Eric out to the St. and got Letter from Edith, Ma, Esther and John Swanes and Magrethe and William. Cooked the bluefin I got from Rude and lawyer liver. Took nap in the P.M. Went to the rocks—three 3 lbs. McCormick 0.

Monday June 27th

Up at 8 A.M. after 11 hrs Sleep—It is blowing a Northerly gale and no fishing weather up to noon. Then it got calm and we made preparations to go out, but suddenly the wind increased from the S.W. and blew a gale in the afternoon.

Then we decided to take a trip in the "Almida" to the Brooktrout hole in Siskiwit Bay. Had a strenuous trip in there against the wind and choppy sea. No fish, then home again and the "Almida" behaved splendidly in the choppy sea.

Had fried redfin for dinner and boiled ditto for Supper—Oh my! What delicious fish. Eleanora fell in and Roy fished her out.

Tuesday June 28th

11 hours sleep again,—up at 8 A.M. Wind blowing a Southwest gale all night, and increasing with threatening clouds—look like a big thunder Squall or rainstorm (noon).

Made Rude a "landing Net" for corks. Wrote letter to John, card to Paulene.

The gale moderated a little in the late P.M. so I took a spin in the "Almida" to the rocks trolling but not a bite, by heck.

Started a downpour after supper and it looks like rain for the rest of the night. Well, the Shack don't leak so what the heck do I care. It's now 7:40 so I am going to roll right in this very moment—let it rain!

Wednesday June 29th 1932

Nice warm day but windy on the lake and we went out to the Rocks early in the morning but owing to the choppy sea and wind we turned back without fishing.

Sent letter to Clar, John and Ma & ET Also got provision ordered with Eric. Got letters from Halloran, E.T. & Abe. In the afternoon we took a trip out to try out trolling first at the point where I caught an 8 lbs.

Then Roy & El went to Redfin Island and tried it out there but not a bite. I later got a 3 lbs. in the Bay.

The wind died out to a dead calm toward Sunset, and it looks good for tomorrow. Trout Skulls For Supper

Thursday June 30th

Good thing it's not boat day to day! 6 A.M. started to blow up a storm from the East and a steady down pour of rain. Boy! The reefs are breaking today, I'll say. The worst blow I have seen here, and at noon it is still in its fury.

Well, I made fire in the old Stove, cooked myself a good cup of coffee, which together with a rug Kavring* put new life in me, so I am O.K.

By heck this Storm is the worst I have ever seen here in my 15 years up here. It is still raging at sun down. Big thunderstorm now raging. Great Scott! What a day! Wrote Several letters—Nils Jensen, Edith, Alice. Card to L. Peterson, Frank, letter to Austgen.

Friday July 1st

Up 6 A.M. The wind has shifted to the North but blowing a gale, and we are in for another bummy day. Barometer away down.

Had a bad night with my stomach. Must have overloaded it last night.

Ha, ha! The Barometer is rising. Hurrah! The Storm will soon be over. And we can get out again.

Eleanora is giving Roy a hair cut; That ought to be a good sign on the Weather Map.

Wrote letter to Cousin Anne, Halloran, Swanes, card to Cliff. John Larson and Chas Bartem and Esther.

Weather Moderating, and it looks a little better. So let's hope tomorrow will be a good fish day. Wind going down and sky clearing.

Saturday July 2nd 1932
Went to the Rocks and tried it out. Not a bloomin bite. Then home for coffee. and at 11:45 set out for Malone Island. John not home. Got drink of Home brew from Benson. Then to Siskiwit Lake. Had lunch on shore. No brooktrout in river

Met John in middle of Bay. Wind (Sowest) increasing and sea got rough. Motor on blink about 11/2 mile from shore. Rowed distance to Paul island, fixed motor there, then bucking a stiff S.W. and choppy sea across channel. Reached home about sundown all tuckered out. I tell you it was heavenly to roll in the soft bunk and close your eyes for a sound sleep after this strenuous day.

Sunday, July 3rd
Up 4:30. Nice calm Morning. Roy and I went out trolling, Roy to Rocks reef and I to McCormick's. No fish. Wind blow up from the Noreast and sea got choppy so we turned our nose homeward. In the afternoon the wind calmed down and we took a spin out to Redfin and Santoriam Reefs* but nary a bite.

Were invited to Rude's for a swell feed of goodies topped off with a big dish of delicious ice cream. So the day was not spent in idleness by any means. Well, tomorrow is the fourth of July so we will probably have another Strenuous day.

4th of July, 1932 – Hurrah!
Went to Hay Bay and there met Mr & Mrs. Sivert Anderson,* the "Strawberry," Ed Kvalvik, Albert Bjorvek and some tourists. Had some good home

brew. Then come John S. with Mr. Johnson and Mr. Benson and Ed Ronning from Malone Island. Then the party set out for Chippewa Harbor where we celebrated the day and night in Dancing, Music, and a spirited fight between Johnson* (a Smålending*) and Young Adam, a 1/4 breed Indian, and in the Melee Holgar Johnson's wife was knocked out by Adam and received a black eye. Surely had a big time. Had plenty of home brew and a barrel of fun.

Holger Johnson and wife

Mrs Sivert Anderson and daughter

Tuesday July 5th

Well, this is the Morning after the 4th. Got up about 5:30 and walked around the bay, up the hill, and then down to Holgar Johnson's House where I met Otto Olson.* While there got a dizzy spell, and he dragged me up to the shack and put me to bed. All in—thought I would cash in, but soon got O.K. again.

The party left Chippewa Harbor about 10 o'clock for Malone Island. Had breaded pork Chops at John Skadberg's. Then in a stiff N.E. we set out for Seg's Harbor. The sea running high across the bay. Arrived home safely. Had coffee, then John, Ed and Adam returned to Malone via Hay Bay.

Wednesday July 6th

A bummy, Chilly day. Wind blowing steadily from the NorEast and the lake was pretty rough. No fishing weather. Roy and I sawed up a lot of logs and monkeyed around the burg. Received letter from Edith and Card from Eric. Also package of sweets from Esther and a letter from her. Also a bundle of Newspapers.

Had baked whitefish for supper and Eleanora fixed it up fine with dressing, and I tell you it slid down without stopping.

Thursday, July 7th

Got up about 6 A.M. and monkeyed around fixing up the boat. Wind calming down so I went to McCormick's and picked up 5 Nice fish – one 20 pounder; one 7 and 5; two 3 1/2 pds. Stayed out there till about 3:30 pm. from 12 – 3:30.

Roy and El went into the Bay and caught two 3 1/2 pds. So this Makes it 7 caught today. Had a dandy 2 1/2 lbs. for Supper and we got away with all but a little piece.

It feels good to get out and get fish again after nearly 2 weeks of bad weather, gayeties, etc. Rolled in about 7:45. Good Nite.

Friday July 8th

Rolled out of bunk at 4:30 A.M. and went over and roused the Newlyweds out. Roy was already up and started to prepare breakfast. So into the boats and off for McCormick's. Wind increasing. Trolled a while. Hooked up one—lost it. Hooked up another– an 18 pounder. Then rowed ashore, fixed Motor, had lunch. Now SW. wind blowing hard and sea choppy. Coasted strenuously on the big swells all the way home.

Wind blowing all afternoon. No trolling. took a nap in the P.M. and felt pretty good. Nice warm day on shore. Bright sunshine.

Saturday, July 9th 1932

A queer Morning. Looked threatening with a dark blue bank in the NorEast. Didn't roll out till 7. Then at 7:30 rowed out to the Rocks reef and caught a 16 pds. and a 3 pds.

The wind blew up and I coasted home to find Roy and El had been out in the Bay and caught a 12 pds and a 6 pds. They thought they had it on me but I beat them by 1 lb. Lunch. Out in the Bay again. I caught 2 More which Made the days catch 44 pd. rd.

During the Night a fierce Rain and Electrical Storm came along. The Thunder & Lightning was awful, and the great downpour of rain put everything in the boat floating.

Sunday, July 10

The day started with a warm Sun and a slight S.W. breeze. Roy and I started for the Rocks but Engine refuse to pump, so we headed (by oar) for the Point and trolled there for some time without success. Then Wind started to blow a gale and we rowed home.

Went out to the "Winyah" with Rude and got Mail from Clarence ("Hoozis"*), John, Hose and Peterson. (Typo.) Egkild Also Newspapers from Esther. and Pkges for Roy & El. Sent letters to Ma, Esther, Clar, William, and "Visergutten."

The day was ideal on shore—sunshiny and warm but blowing a gale on lake. The Winyah surely did the "highland fling" on the big swells.

Had a shipment of 76 lbs.

Monday July 11th
Another windy Morning. Went to the Rock reef and Roy and El got one little squibb of 2 lbs – Nice little "Kogefisk." I got 0.

Then wind changed to SoWest. And we rolled home hungry and disgusted.

Wind kept blowing all day and weather threatening.

El picked Strawberries and we had each a fine dish for our supper lunch.

Roy fixed the motor pump so now we hope our troubles will be over. Wrote letter to Egkild. Mosquitoes and Blackflies are bad actors—

Tuesday July 12th 1932
Man oh Man! Such weather! A solid downpour all night and a terrible electrical storm, together with wind and sea, like an October storm.

Rain continued half of the day.

John Skadberg came along in his fishing boat late in the afternoon and we had dinner together.

In the morning I made fire in the stove and it felt mighty fine. Wrote letter to Jak Larson and Ma (check), also wrote to Edith and Alice "Weakly Hoozis."

It looks threatening and we may have more bad weather. The Barometer is falling and the Lord knows What's gone to be!

Wednesday, July 13th

A fair quiet morning and somewhat of a trolling day. I went to McCormick's about 7:30 and caught a nice 25 lbdr. and returned home at 11:15 and shipped it on the Str. together with a 3 lbdr. Roy & L caught. In the afternoon I returned to McCormick's for a few hours and caught another 25 lbdr. That made it a fair day's fishing.

Got a letter from Halloran and one from Ma telling about the tense Chicago conditions and that Otto was liable to be laid off.

The "tapeworm" on my table is still wriggling around in the milk bottle. Had a whopper trouthead for Supper.

Thursday, July 14th

Up at 5 g.m. and woke the newlyweds. Had breakfast and I started off for McCormick's again to hook up another cow, and sure enough—caught another 25 1/2 redfin—a fine fish. This makes the 3d 25 lbs. in succession. Roy and L went to the Bay and caught a 5 lbs. We all got back for dinner. Then it started to blow and no more fishing for today. Took a nap and the rain pelting the roof of my shack woke me up. Made fire in my stove and took it easy for the rest of the day. Raw and nasty out. Bum weather approaching (?) Barometer is going down!

Friday July 15th

Well, the bummy weather is here again with a chilly fog and it rained good and plenty last night and a chilly N.E. Wind.

Cleared up a little towards noon and I went to the Point and not a blame bite. Wind and sea moderated a little so Roy and I went to the Rocks and McCormick's. Then a heavy fog drifted in and a strong wind (S.E.) came along and we beat it for home. The fog was so thick that we could hardly see shore 5 yards away. And it is still thick fog at bed time. No fish today.

Saturday July 16th

Foggy and chilly morning. Fog lifted and the hot sun came forth. Souwest blew up. Went to the Bay with Roy and L and trolled around the point. Wind increased to a young gale. I caught a 7 pounder at the Point. Rowed ashore and had lunch. Then rowed home against a choppy sea. Spring in water pump busted. Roy fixed up another. Mrs. Rude brought over fish cake and fruit supe and it was fine. Flies are terrible. A hot day, but no fishing weather. Fine day on shore (except for flies) but windy on the lake. Letter to Otto, Carson, Edith and Abe. Papers to Andreas.

Sunday, July 17th

The motor got on the bum again last night. So I got up at 5 am and rowed out to the Rocks without breakfast as I didn't care to wake the N.W. Rowed around for 3 hrs. without a fish. Then home and cooked coffee. Roy & L still sleeping at 9 o'clock. A nice calm morning Would like to be at Mc-Cormick now.

Went to the Point. Nothing doing. Tried the channel reef. Got 4 nice trout one 16 lb; one 10 lb; one 7 lb.; one 5 lb. Roy and L went to Redfin and caught 2; one 7 lb; one 6 lb. I went fishing without breakfast. Received mail from Edith, Alice and Clar. "Hoozis" All good cheerful news. Had a shipment of 80 lbs. A record breaker So far. Roy and I caught another 5 pounder.

Monday, July 18th

One of the nicest—in fact the nicest Mornings since we came here. Got up at 5 and started at 6 for McCormick's reefs. Arrived there at 7 o'clock and trolled all morning without a bite.

Disgusted and tired we set the motor a going and went to Long Point. Reached there 12 noon and Mosied around, had lunch and started back at 1:45. Trolled the reefs on way home—nothing doing. Then for home sweet home, arr. at 5 o'clock. Had supper: Boiled Trout and Spuds, Bread, Tea and Plum sauce. I eat 4 piece of fish and it tasted fine.

Tuesday, July 19th

Oh what different day this is from yesterday. Started for a trolling trip to Redfin. Then met John. Dark blue cloud formed in West and then we rowed to Paul Island for Shelter; there John joined us and it started to pour down terribly with lightning and thunder. Then after a little let up we motored home. Then it started with a down pour again and kept raining and a fog all the rest of the day. Had fire in stove and felt comfy. El baked doughnuts and we had coffee and swatted flies. Finished up #2 "Fish Scale". Took a nap.

Wednesday July, 20

One measly miserable foggy morning. Last night the rain came down in torrents with vivid flashes of lightning and terrible peals of thunder. When I came down to the dock I discovered that the boats were actually half full of rain water.

Went out with Rude in a blinding fog to the Winyah. Hard job to locate her. Got vacuum bottle from home, letter from Swaves and E.T. Foggy all day. Roy and L went berry picking. Came back with two big dishes full of strawberries which we had for supper together with flapjocks, tea and good bread. Chilly and raw outdoors. 7 to 8 inches.

Thursday, July 21

An extraordinary hot clear sunshiny day on shore, but blowing a Souwest gale. Tried out trolling, but no good. Hooked up a small kogefisk but lost it—darn it.

Bucked the strong wind from the point home with the Elto full speed and staid home the rest of the day. Took nap in P.M. and worked on the "Scale" awhile. Had a big dish of strawberries for lunch.

The fishermen are getting hardly no fish on their nets and it look skimpy for the trolling hook. Hope tomorrow will be a good day.

Friday July 22d 1932

Nice morning but wind blowing strongly from North

Slept till 8 o'clock and didn't disturb the newlyweds. Cooked coffee in my shack and had lunch.

Mosied around until the wind calmed down about 3 P.M., then Roy and I started out trolling. Roy got 0 and I caught a 10 pounder and a 2 1/2 lb kogefisk which we had for supper.

Saturday July 23d

A nice calm morning. Up at 6 and woke R & El. Had a big bunch of swell Fl. Jocks for breakfast. Then started for a trolling day. Went down the F.H. reefs and caught 2. Then to Redfin. Met Ed Holte* and he towed me to Harlem Reefs. There I caught 3 small ones and a 20 pounder— 6 in all. Roy & L went to the lt. house and I went home with the fish, then back to Paul Islands when I met R & L and towed them back home. They had caught no

Ed Holte

fish. After sup, we went out again—no fish

Sunday July 24th

This is boat day. and it rained this morning so I didn't get up till 6 o'clock. Cooked coffee all by myself and had a lonesome light lunch. Then woke Roy and went out trolling. Got a 1 1/2 lb whopper which we had for dinner. In P.M. went to Santoriam and Harlem reefs but not a bite. Roy and El got two 2lb squibbs in the bay

Received letter from Ma and Edith and "Hoozis" from Clar and Esther.

Shipped 33 lbs. fish.

It turned out to be a swell warm sunshiny day.

El baked a swell 3 Story cake.

Monday July 25th

This is a regular Blue Monday indeed. A pouring rain pelting the roof at 5 A.M. and, accompanied by thunder and lightning, kept up all day long with a heavy thick fog for dressing. If we ever have had a joykilling day this one caps the climax. Sat in my lonely hut all day except at meal time over with Roy and El. Wrote letter to E.T., Ma, Eric, and finished up #3 "Scale."

Had fire in stove all day to keep away the gloom and raw air. Mamaman! When will we get decent weather? Never saw the boat.

Tuesday July 26

Well, it rained again during night and occasionally some damn thing would land on the roof, scratching and making noise that kept me awake. Maybe an owl. Got up at 7 A.M. The wind blowing a gale from the North and No fishing weather. Made myself a cup of coffee. Took a shave—shaved off the "brush".

Wind went down in the P.M. and we went trolling. Roy & El to the Rocks caught 5 fish: 6, 5, 4, 3, 2. I didn't get any. So they beat me again. I went to McCormick's.

Strawberries for dinner & Supper. The wind went down to a dead calm.

Wednesday, July 27

Nice and calm at Sunrise. Got out of bunk at 5.30 and woke Roy and after Breakfast we went to the Rocks. Roy caught 1 at Boat Harbor. I got 0. Then wind blew up and we for home, then it began raining and foggy. Shipped 18 pounds of fish

Late in P.M. we went out to the Point & Bay. Roy and L caught one 2 lbs and one 1 lbs. I caught a 2 1/2 lbs.

Had peasup for Supper. Received Springs from Clar, and 2 boxes of caramels from Esther.

Weather tonight looks like rain on the program.

Thursday, July 28

Rained again last night. Up at 6 and out at 7. Had flopjack for B.F. Then went trolling down along the reef and Point. Roy & L went to Redfin but wind blew up so they came back to the point and I towed them home. Late in P.M. went to the Point and Bay. I caught 3 small ones and Roy & El caught 4 —. So the day yielded 7 in all. 3-3-2 for E.A. and 5-3-3-2 for R. & El.

The weather in the afternoon became threatening and choppy in the Bay. I loaded up my boat with fire logs and brought them home. Roy and El came home quite late, but in good spirits at beating me again.

Friday July 29th

Roy, El, and I went to the Rocks reef trolling. R & L got 0 and I got one little 2 pounder, then I went to McCormick's rowing nearly all the way but not a fish. There the wind blew up strong and I coasted all the way home from McCormick in the heavy S.W.

The wind kept on steady all afternoon so it became a bum day on the lake but a hot day on shore.

I told the kids that I was going trolling early tomorrow morning.

Saturday, July 30th

Well, I kept my word and got up at 5 am. Cooked myself a cup of Java and after a hasty lunch I jumped into my overalls and boat and out to the Point caught one little squibb, then to the reef where I caught 7. Then home for lunch and out again. Caught 1 on the point and one on the reef.

That makes 10 for today. Roy and El didn't get any. Total Wt. Round 25 1/2 lbs. Dressed 20 lbs.

The biting flies are terrible today. We had a rain shower late in P.M. Troll kjerringen* is out early and late—she is fish crazy—absolutely.

Sunday, July 31st

A very calm morning. Got Up at 5 A.M. cooked myself a cop of coffee and a Wheat Biscuit and out I went to the reefs. Trolled around for 3 hrs. without a bite. Roy and El got one 3 pounder in the Bay.

Had a shipment of 30 lbs. on the Winyah.

Eleanora baked the 3 pounder—a fine redmeated fish.

This is a fine sunny day with a light breeze from the N.E. I went to Harlem and got 2—4 and 3 1/2. Roy & El to the Rocks got 7 trls. 8 1/2, 7 1/2, 5 1/2, 3 1/2, 2 1/2, 1.

Monday, Aug 1st

The Mo. of Aug. is starting pretty good. A fine morning and me up at 6. Made a hasty lunch and out to the Rocks and caught 3. Then home for dinner. Took a nap after lunch and at 3 P.M. went to the reefs and Point. Caught 3 More. 11, 4, 2, 3, 3, 2. 6 in all

Roy and El went to the Rocks in the P.M., caught one 3 lbs. Wind and sea started and they went to Boat Harbor for safety, started walking home but changed their mind and came along motoring in the heavy sea at 1/2 speed. Rude and I went after them in his boat and met them 1/2 way down.

Tuesday, Aug. 2nd

The Barometer is going down, indicating rough weather and it's raining, and rough on the Lake. Up at 8 A.M. Made fire in the old rusty stove. Steady downpour, and the reefs are breaking furiously. The fog is covering the hillside.

Rained pretty nearly all day except at 6 P.M. The sun came peeping through the Western sky and cheered us up a bit. I hope tomorrow will be a nice day so we can get out and catch a dinner fish before the Winyah comes. Wrote to Edith J. and Edith Seglem for coffee, also finished up #4 of the "Scale." No fishing today

Wednesday Aug 3rd

Of course it rained in the morning, but I took a trip out to the Point before the boat came and hooked up a nice 12 pound whopper, which will help our shipment on today's boat.

Sam Rude

Roy went out with Rudes to the Winyah and got the Mail—letter from Ma, papers from S., and letter from Chas. Seglem

Had a shipment of 54 lbs @ 9 ¢.

Thursday Aug 4

Rain again off and on during the day. Took a trip to McCormick's to try it out—Nothing doing. Trolled the Rock reefs. Same results. Tried the Point and Bay. Not a bite. Snapped a 3 pounder at the Reefs. Roy and L went to the Rocks in the P.M. and caught a 10 pounder and a 2 1/2 lbs.

A bad looking rain cloud drew up from the N. W. and with lightning and Thunder bursted about 9 P.M.

We had raspberry jam and sauce for supper. Berry picked at Boat Harbor and around here.

Friday Aug 5, 1932

Will it rain again today? Certainly. Got up about 7 o'clock and woke the NW and after a bumper breakfast of flapjacks and bacon I set out for the point for a tryout. Then Roy & El came along—No fish

To the 5 mile beach for raspberries. Found a canful. Then motored home. Weather looked ugly and squally, and started a downpour with thunder & Lightning right after we got home. Had fried trout for dinner.

Roy gave me a haircut. John Skadberg was here in our absence.

A squally and no-good trolling weather.

Had delicious raspberry Pie for supper.

Saturday Aug 6th
To begin with we simply say: Rain Rain go away—come again Some other day—enuff sed!

When it moderated I took a Spin in the Almida to the Rocks and got Nothing. Then to Boat Hrbr and picked a can of Raspberries then home. Roy and El went to the Bay and got a 3 lb Koge fisk which we had for Supper. I tried out the reef but lost the Rude Spoon.* Then after I got home we had another rain shower.

Saw a flock of 8 cranes making for Boat Harbor

Another squally rainy day—

Sunday, Aug 7th
Of course it rained! Showers only. Went out on the reef to look for my Spoon but too windy, couldn't see it.

Picked some blueberries, went to the Steamer and got the cake Nursie Anna* sent. Received "Hoozis." Got a box from E.T. with Peaches, Plums, Tomatoes and Coffee, also letter saying the fish I sent was received and appreciated. We soon had a feast of dinner with all those goodies and we were indeed glad to get all that good stuff.

Monday, Aug 8th
The same old Grind, out in the wind and rain. Between the puffs and showers we picked Blueberries and kept from stagnation the best we could.

No fishing. I tried out the Rock reefs but the wind and sea got the best of me.

Tuesday Aug 9th
A beautiful calm morning and us out trolling.

Roy went down the reefs toward Redfin Island and I to the Rock reef. Roy picked up 4— 2 1/4, 2 1/3, 1 3/4, 5 1/4 lbs.

I caught 4 also— 2 1/2, 4 3/4, 1 3/4, 1 1/2 lbs. This makes 8 for the day

Started out for the Rocks again in the P.M., but it got pretty rough and we went to Boat Harbor and picked Raspberries and Blueberries.

And of course it rained again today.

Had a Vegetarian Supper

Wednesday, 10/1932
XXXXXXXX Knock Wood, an ideal day.

Best day as far as weather goes we have had this summer.

Out trolling: Roy caught 6 in the morning and 1 in the afternoon— 19 lbs together.

Elling

Dad caught 2 in morning and 6 in afternoon—20 1/2 lbs.

Had a 28 lb shipment

No rain!

Thursday Aug 11.
Fine day. but although we tried our damest to hook up some fish our efforts were in vain.

To the Reefs, Point Rock, and McCormick's, but no fish.

I hooked up a 3 pounder coming home, but in landing him I slung him across the boat, and he fell off the hook and disappeared on the other side of the boat and I stood there like getting slapped in the face.

No rain!

Friday Aug 12

A most perfect day. Warm and Sunshiny all day. And absolutely calm on the water except for a little breeze toward noon.

To the reefs—Nothing doing.

To the Point—caught a 4 lbs.

Then to Harlem reefs I caught a 1 1/2 lbs. and Roy caught four 2 pds. That makes it 6 for the day.

Had 2 big dishes of beautiful rice for supper. Hope it agrees with my stomach.

No rain! Knock wood!

Saturday Aug. 13

An ideal day. Went trolling and got 0.

Took a trip to Malone Island and on the way back stopped at Wright's Island, and got motor fixed.

Then we had a wonderful trip across the glassy moonlit Siskiwit Bay. Made the trip from Wright's Island to Seglems Harbor in 1 hour and 10 m. Got home at 9^{00} P.M.

Sunday, Aug. 14

A very fine day, although a little windy.

Went out trolling but 0. Guess it's played out for good.

Roy went out the Str. and bt. 2 lbs butter and got mail, Newspapers from S. the "Hoozis" from Clar and letter from Edith and Esther.

Then we went blueberry picking and got quite a bit.

Sh. 20 lbs— The Washington Harbor fishermen stopped in on their way to Chippewa Harbor. Some went to Duluth.

Monday. Aug 15

A windy threatening day. John Skadberg came over from Malone Island for a visit and staid over night. In the evening we played cards and had a nice time in general. Everybody happy.

No fishing. Trolling is absolutely austgespielt.*

Tuesday August 16

The weather is nice and exceptionally hot. 77° in the Shade.

Got up early and set Roy's flap jack factory abuzzing.

Woke the boys for breakfast and then they left for the lake and Malone Island.

I tried out trolling but 0. Roy and El caught a little kogefish and we fried it for supper.

Wednesday Aug 17th

Nice morning. Warm and genial. Did a little packing together of little odds and ends. Will soon be on our way to home.

Sent letter to Zoeller and "Visergutten," also the "Scale."

Big bull moose swimming in the bay.

Got big 9 lb lawyer from Rude.

Roy went out to Winyah to get the battery.

We did a little packing and preparing for leaving as soon as possible.

Big Noreaster blowing and it looks ugly.

Thursday Aug 18

A roaring gale has been blowing from the Noreast all night and is still blowing.

Made up my account and found it as follows:

Fish	47.12
less Schrinking	2.49
	44.63
Gass 35 gals.	7.30
bal.	37.33

The barometer is going up. Good weather ahead—

Wind calming down towards evening

Picked Blueberries

Friday Aug 19
Well we have completed packing and now to get started on the home going.

The Southwest as usual is blowing and we can't get away.
—Everything ready.

Packed the stuff in the Almida and after everything was all set —here comes John Skadberg and the Wright Isl. people in their boat to visit us. They stuck around and had coffee then good night. Also said goodbye to the Rudes—Good nite, Fisherman's Home

Fisherman's Home

Saturday Aug 20
Up at 3³⁰ and at 4 A.M. started off for Washington Harbor. Long Point* at 6, left L.P. 6:30 A.M., WH 8 A.M. Met Siv., then to Johnson Island and had lunch—then to Club House, then to Gills—bt potatoes & fish—to J Isle, for

fish, cookt spuds on Offer pst—Slept—them prchs load of bals boughs—
had coffee—Hit the balsom bunk and called it a day. Felt pretty good and
everybody happy, and was soon off to dreamland

Sea rough from the S.W. gale but dying down at night.

Sunday. Aug 21st
Started from W.H. at 2:45 A.M. The lake was fairly calm except for heavy
swells from yesterday.

The Moon shone brightly and the going was good except for pump trouble,
but Roy overcame that. Set the course Northwest from Johnson Island and
arrived at Susie Island* at 6:30. Then stopped there and had lunch. Then
proceeded along the North Coast till 9 A.M. when the SW blew into a gale
and we had to put in at Rocky Point* for shelter. Then we made ourselves
"at home" in an empty house. Picked blueberries and put up over night.
Watched the Winyah pass at 7 pm. Hit the bunk at sundown.

Monday Aug 22
After a little nap in that strange empty house at Rocky Point we woke at 2
A.M., cooked coffee, and packed our duds in the "Almida" and at 3 A.M. in a
beautiful moonlight and calm sea pointed our nose westward and off for
our destination Grand Marais. Good going. Sea calm, but heavy swells. At
"5-Mile Rock*" a heavy fog bank swallowed us up and we had to hug the
shore all the rest of the way. Arrived at Grand Marais at 9 A.M. and met the
Seglems who had been waiting for us since yesterday.

Roy fixed car and Chas. & Johnny entertained us in evening. Mr. & Mrs.
Mackew called and we had a pleasant evening at Chas. Seglem's. Stayed
there during the night.

Tuesday Aug 23
Had a good night's sleep and felt fine. A big stack of flop jacks awaited our
big appetite.

Left Grand Marais at 10 am. for William's at Bev Bay.* Arrived there a little
after noon.

Visited the Palisade Blueberry hill* in the afternoon and picked a lot of berries. Met Gertie and her kid.

Got a good dinner and fine supper and felt fine although a little bit tired.

Listened to old Bill talking politics and had a good time.

Wednesday Aug 24
Went to the Blueberry hill again and picked till 1 P.M. Then cleaned up and made preparations to depart for Duluth. Started for Duluth at 4^{15} pm. Heavy rainstorm between K.R.* and Dul. Arrived at Duluth at 5:30 and got our affairs with Christiansen* fixed up in good shape. Then had a good lunch after which we went to E.T. and Fraunk's. Roy & El. staid at Fraunk's at nite. I slept with E.T.

Felt pretty good and everybody happy.

Thursday Aug 25
Left Duluth for Chicago at 8:30 A.M. and drove all day and all night until 3 A.M. when we stopped at 4514 tired, sleepy and weary but glad that the long journey was at an end, and that everything had gone good and with no mishaps, punctures, or other things to mar a most wonderful and novel trip.

rfp!

Elling, Roy and Eleanora
lunching on beach

Found everybody well and happy at home.

Found everybody well and happy at home

143

The Fish Scale

ITS ALLRITE IN ITS WAY — BUT IT DON'T WEIGH MUCH

VOL. 1. SEGLEM'S HARBOR, JULY 10, 1932 NO. 1.

The Roy A. Seglems Will Honeymoon at Isle Royale

The wedding of Roy A. Seglem of 4514 N. Troy St. and Miss Eleanor Nelson, daughter of Mr. and Mrs. Martin Nelson of Elburn, Illinois, was celebrated at the home of the bride's parents at Elburn last Saturday. The Rev. Mr. Glad of Geneva tied the matrimonial knot. The young couple will spend their honeymoon at Seglem's Harbor, Isle Royale, Uncle Sam's latest acquired national park, in Lake Superior, where Mr. Seglem has a fishing station and summer cabin.

"Hoozis" This?

Several days ago we had the great hilarious pleasure of receiving the foist copy of "The Weakley(?) Hoozis" edited by the able writer and well-known scientific philosopher Clarence Algernon Seglem assisted in the culinary department by the most efficient Co-Ed and kitchen mechanic Esther Hilda Jeanette Seglem. We welcome this pappy and snappy "raglan" into our fold. It has been the sad means of inspiring us to the mad desperation and exasperation of creating "The Fish Scale" and hope with body and sole that we may have the pleasure of exchanging (like Sharkey and Schmelling*) blow for blow in the publishers' sanctum. We thank thee, Ed and Co-Ed, for your efforts in our behalf and wish to congratulate you on your first No. and shall await with great pleasure the next one.

4ths on the Isle

With the family "coat of arms," the pretty pennant pleasantly waving from the bow and the glorious stars and stripes floating from the stern the proud ship "ALMIDA" started off from Seglem's Harbor at 10:30 a.m. for Hay Bay, 3 1/2 miles across Siskiwit Bay, on the morning of July 4th to participate in the great Fisherman's Festivities scheduled to take place at Chippewa Harbor, 18 miles by boat to the east. In our party were Eleanora and Roy and the old leatherneck E.A. Before we started we had put under our belts a mountain of delicious flapjacks which put pep and unbounded expectations in our happy party.

At Hay Bay we were welcomed with open arms by Mr. and Mrs. Sivert Anderson and Ed Kvalvick and a bunch of Chicago and New York tourists. Then Mr. Albert Bjorvek came skidding in to the Bay in his skiff at a speed of 15 miles p.h. His little craft on an angle of and with full speed ran high and dry on the beach. Old Albert was feeling gay—had a grin on his face which would have gladdened the heart of the most sourbellied crab. He had several bottles of swell home brew in his boat and of course we all had to sample it, and to tell the truth, it was the best home brew I have ever tasted.

Then along about 11 a.m. comes John Skadberg in his boat the "Bess" and we scrambled into his boat and set off for Malone Island about 6 miles to the east. There we went ashore and had lunch. (Eleanora had put up a big box full of goodies that we had taken along.) Here we left-

(continued on next page)

4th on the Isle

(Continued from 1st page)

the good ship "ALMIDA" after towing her from Hay Bay. From Malone Island the party (now augmented to 8 persons viz: John Skadberg, Ed Ronning, Ben Benson, Johnson, Ed Kvalvik, Roy and Eleanora and E.A. Also old Bjorvek in his speedy skiff) set off in the "Bess" and the "Slim" for Chippewa Harbor about 8 miles to the east.

With the stars and stripes flying high overhead the speedy "Bess" plowed on and after an hour's motoring and gayety on the smooth surface of Lake Superior along the rock hewn shore we finally entered the beautiful Chippewa Harbor channel.

At Holger Johnson's dock we were welcomed by a crowd of merry makers who had come from different fishing stations to help the Johnson family celebrate the Fourth of July. Then more people from Wright's Island, Rock Harbor, Park Place,* Tourist Home,* and adding our party from Seglem's Harbor, Siskiwit Bay, Hay Bay and Malone Island, made a formidable crowd of men, women, and children.

Well, folks, we had the time of our life, music, singing, dancing, eating, good beer, fighting and ev'rything that goes to make up a real celebration.

A Swede from Wright's Island who boasted that he had licked a large number of Polacks at Green Bay got snotty with a halfbreed Indian and started a fight which ended with the "terrible Swede" being knocked out and thrashed good and plenty. During the pleasantries, Mrs. Holger Johnson tried to interfere and was herself knocked flat on the ground, receiving a wallop in the eye which put a peach of a 4th of July decoration on her map. But she came up smiling and declaring that if they did not behave themselves, she would clean up the whole dam bunch.

Dad's Daily Duty

At the Door of the Newly weds.

Notes of the Party

Roy and Dad got a bawling out from Old man Bjorvek because Roy couldn't understand Norwegian.

Ed Kvalvik wore a cap resembling a tent and also wore a broad grin when he drank home brew.

Eleanora said she never had a more enjoyable 4th of July.

Pity the poor smalenning. He got trimmed to perfection by the Red man. And he still wears the decorations.

Old man Bjorvek danced every dance on the program and didn't fish for 3-4 days afterwards.

On the way back we had breaded pork chops at John Skadberg's at his shack at Malone Island.

Bjorvek sure has a speedy boat and his Home Brew has a lot of pep too.

Some of the Fishermen did not go out on the lake to fish(?) for several days afterwards.

Mr. & Mrs. Holger Johnson are surely great and hospitable people. They provided sleeping quarters for all of us.

HEP! HEP!

WOTTA LIFE! WOTTA LIFE!

Roy in the pleasant act of preparing a hasty meal. We have 3 square meals a day—Oatmeal, Cornmeal and Fish.

We have

Oatmeal, C.

Notice to Our Readers:
The Fish Scale don't come off regularly so don't be disappointed if you have to wait.

? Unanswerable

Little Joan Skadberg (3 years old) came over to Eleanora one evening and among a number of childish questions asked:
"What you goin to do now?"
Eleanora:"Go to bed."
Joan:"What you goin to do then?
Eleanora:"Go to sleep."
Joan:"What you goin to do then?"
Eleanora:_____! (stumped)

Crazy Pete has nothing on the hard boiled fishermen up here they can open the bottles with their teeth too.

Teeth too.

The other day I prepared fish for dinner and left the dish of fish right outside the cabin door, and went down to the fish house on the dock. The gulls swooped down on the fish and Eleanora picked up a big rock and threw it with might and main in the direction of the gulls but it landed with tremendous force where I stood and bounced away out into the lake. Lucky for me that it missed me or I would now be in the hospital.

Red as a lobster fine as a fish
In this wilderness bosom I'm dwelling—
But something is lacking and this is my wish:
That Almida was here with her Elling.

THE WEATHER

Fine and warm on shore but bummy, windy, rainy, cold, foggy on the lake most of time otherwise R-O-T-T-E-N.

otherwise R-O-T-T-E-N.

A Regular Hangout

Here you have Mrs. Seglem Jr. in the act of hanging out Roy's B.V.D.s and other ornaments. Whether it is an act of charity or necessity or purely an act of mad desperation, we do not know, but as far as we are concerned, we don't indulge in such foolishness only but once a month whether we need to or not.

Darn his old socks anyhow!!!

THE FISH SCALE

Odds and Evens

We picked up a moose horn the other day weighing 12 pounds and measuring from tip to base 34 1/2 inches. Some horn!

No. 2 of the Weakly Hoozis thankfully (not tankfully) received and is intensely interesting. Great idea, Clarence. But what became of your Co-Ed? Did you leave your able assistant down on the farm or did you throw her into the Hell Box?

Have written Larson.

Weasels are killing rabbits right under our nose.

The delicious sweet wild strawberries are now ripe and we have each of us a dish of the dainty morsels for supper nearly every day.

Gosh old Fish hooks! If you folks could only sit at our table and get some of that swell redmeated trout for dinner! Mmm! Mmm!

Hope the weather will soon moderate so we can get out after the big ones at McCormick's.

Black (Blood) flies crawled into Roy's shirt and down on his stomach. On the way down they made two nice bites on his chest between his Katti patta. Nice round and souvenirs to be proud of.

I had a letter from Chicago stating that the printing business is in a terrible mess. That the out of work benefits have been stopped and that the union is in an uproar, and over 1600 printers going idle. I am glad I am here, even though it's stormy.

The wings and claws of this boid will soon adorn th back porch at 4514. They are now ornamenting Seglem's cabin together all kinds of other junk

Snap Shots

Poor Roy—please pity him he has lost his appetite. He could eat only eleven flapjacks this morning.

Ha ha ha! "He who laughs last laughs best." Roy and Eleanora thought they had it on me the other day. I went to the Rocks trolling and they to the Bay. They came back home with two fish—a 12-pounder and a 6lbs. and when I came back a little later they stood on the dock grinning—thinking I had nothing. Well, I had two fish also. "We beat you this time, Dad," they said. "We have 18 pounds!" "Fine" says I, "we'll see." Well, I weighed my two and one was 16 lbs. and the other 3 lbs. "All right" says I, "I got you beat by one pound!" "Doggone it, anyhow!" exclaimed Eleanora, "He's bound to beat us!"

Tuesday July 12—A regular September Snorter. A downpour of rain all nite. Fierce thunderstorm and wind blowing a gale from the Noreast. Sea running and reefs breaking with big combers. Joy is completely taken out of life. Oh, for Otto's basement and Vera's home brew!

Political Notes

Hurrah for Roosevelt. Powers be to him. Poor Hoover, he will have lots of time to go fishing after elections.

Things look wet—feel wet, you bet—so does the seat of my pants after a day's fishing.

The fishermen of Isle Royale are all (?) wet—wringing wet—and Home Brew is to be found in nearly every shack.

147

The Fish Scale

IT NEVER GETS WELL IF YOU PICK IT

Vol. 1   Seglem's Harbor, July 20, 1932.   No. 2

A Dam-Damp Trip.

July 19. This morning we made a trip to Redfin Island for the purpose of trolling. When we got there we met John Skadberg and his man. We trolled about half an hour, then a dark blue cloud formed in the West and streaks of lightning could be seen in the clouds. We then hiked for Paul Island for shelter, pulled our boats up and waited for the coming

VERA
AND HER FAMOUS
HB
Home Brew

BAVARIA'S HIGH SPIRITS EXPLAINED.

MUNICH— "No wonder we're ready to go the limit on monarchy when you consider we drink full-strength beer."

Tell her to save some till we get home.

storm. Then John came full speed in his big fishing boat to join us. He has a canvas canopy covering his boat and just as the storm bursted we all scrambled into his boat. Then the rain came down with a roar. And such rain! A veritable cloud burst! But we managed to motor home 3 miles after a letup. And now we're happy. *re happy.*

Items of Interest

Eleanora has a swell little garden of lettuce, radishes, carrots, pansies, etc.

It has been raining all day since we came back from Redfin Isle.

Eleanora made some delicious doughnuts and I have just been over there for DN and coffee. The holes were excellent too.

The flies in John Skadberg's shack were so thick that he had to go outside to eat his meals.

The fog is now so thick us can hardly see across the bay.

I have a beautiful bouquet of Sweet William on my table—picked at Long Point where we were yesterday. *sterday.*

I caught three 25-pounders in succession a few days ago. Hope to repeat it, if not to better it soon. But prospects are poor, and weather steadily against us.

A Letter of Thanks
To the Editor of the Hoozis—

Thanks for the illustration "Dad when in his prime" on the front page of last issue. Very good—I'll say. *I'll say.*

Thanks for the Nuts and Bolts and *nd* spark plug and the brass fitting. *ing.*

Thanks for the newspapers you sent, sweet "Co-Ed". *f Co-Ed.*

Thanks for the clipping about that *it* Stuben Building fire. That must have been a spectacular blaze. *blaze.*

Thanks for your interesting story of the Great Celebration the bunch had down on the farm the 4th. Glad to hear Ma got 1st prize for rolyboly-ing on the lawn. See Hilda displayed everything she had and I guess she's got a lot to show. Oh, Man!

Thanks for the Weakly Hoozis, *is* it is some gloom chaser, I'll say. *ay.* Hope ye Ed and ye Co-Ed will never get tired of sending it. *ught.*

Thanks for the Pennant pole you sent along with Eric. It looks fine on the bow of the "ALMIDA" *w of the ALMIDA"*

And a Couple of Hurrahs for

The The Popular "Co-Ed" of the Hoozis. *We* We have surely been enthused and *d* *en* enticed by her intoxicating articles in *of* *u* that Weakly bladder. But—something *so* has gone kaput. We think the chief *s* *thi* Ed has eliminated or curtailed her *ted* *or curtailed* culinary gizzard. *gizzard.*

OUCH! EVERY TIME I SHAVE, MY FACE FEELS SORE. HOW IT HURTS!

Ro Roy seems to have a strenuous time *ti* keeping his face smooth. And his be-loved better 1/2 is always complaining *complain* of roughness. *hness.* *There* There is a reason (?) (!)—

Cornbeef Nose

Say folks did ye ever hear a Say, folks, did ye ever hear of a cornbeef nose? Well, here is one. We have some cornbeef in a jar in the fish house and I asked El if she thought it was all right yet, whereupon she answered: "Sure, I had my nose in it!" Well, it looks like it—as it is as RED as the rear light on Roy's flivver and it shines like the moon on a cloudy night *on a cloudy night.*

Fish Flakes
Fish or Akes
Fish Fakes

You-ree-kah! I have found it! a petri-
fied peanut.

Eleanora has acquired Treesmag.

A generous mosquito settled on
Roy's Bombasity, helped itself to a
generous meal, and now the poor
gink walks bowlegged.

Eleanor has adopted Jennie's slogan:
"Eat 'em while they're hot."

> When cleaning shrimp always re-
> move the dark streak down the back.

There are a lot of shrimps that ought to
have their yellow strip removed too.
"I shay sho."

"GO TO HELL"

said Roy the other day
when he lost a fish, and
really you can't blame him.

A pretty little song sparrow is sitting
on a twig near my shack and cheers
me every morning with her sweet song.

The fish is biting—lykell—lykell!*
but not on my old hook.

Poletickle Noose

> President Hoover returned to the
> White House late yesterday from his
> fishing camp at Rapidan, Va.

After March 4, 1933,
Mr. Hoover will be
sitting pretty on
his new seat. Here
is a fine conception
of his comfy seat.
We hope it fits nice
and snugly to his
rear monstrosity.

No, this is not
the face of an
Isle Royale
Python. It's
the kissing
apparatus
of a camel.
But who the
L wants to
kiss a camel? No girl would!

We have a bountiful dish of delicious sweet
wild strawberries each for the supper table
almost every evening—and oh, how good!

Oh, if we only
had a mugful
of that delicious
Home Brew made
by that generous
sweet maid
VERA,
wouldn't life
be sweet up
here in this ____
wilderness? Well,
we'll drown ourselves
in it when we get home.

> SLANG TRACED TO ITS SOURCE SPOTS.
>
> "I'm strong for you," said Samson to Delilah.
> "You must come across," Hero told Leander. "I'll
> tell the world!" cried Paul Revere. "Over the
> river," said George Washington, as he tossed the
> dollar. "You're a devil," Proserpina told Pluto.
> "Not so hot," said Shadrach to Meshach and
> Abednego. "It's a great life if you don't weaken,"
> said Atlas. "Beautiful but dumb," observed Na-
> poleon, gazing at the Sphinx.

Our slang goes like this:
slam the sucker mosquito, bing the dam
fly; shut your gab Gull; darn that old stove;
another sour morning! Says *We*.

7/20—Went down to the dock this morning
and discovered that the boat was actually half
filled with rain water from last night's terrible
downpour. I have never seen anything like it.
The fog now is so thick you could almost cut it
with a knife. It sure takes the joy out of life. Well,
we have to take it—that's all!

Here, dear folks, you have a fair conception of Zar Christianson,* captain and whole cheese of the steamer "Winyah," who has said he will see that the fishermen of Isle Royale shall not earn their salt this summer. He has the monopoly of the fish business under his thumb and fixes the price of fish as he likes, and if the fishermen don't like it they can go to grass.

Father and Son returning from a successful fishing trip at McCormick's.

With Apologies to Kate Smith*

When Red and Snuspick drink moonshine
Ev'ry drop has a comeback for more,
Again we shall sample their moonshine
In Otto's old basement next door,
In the daytime it's dry and dreary
But the evening is bright and cheery
When Red and Snuspick drink moonshine
I'm thirsty and longing for more!

Drop Case Against Nelson

What kind of a case was it, Otto? Was the case full or empty? Hope it was not very heavy. Tell us something about it please.

Whopee—have anezzer

It sure was great 4th of July celebration the Fisherfolks arranged. Everything in it from an Indian fight to a souse. And Mrs. Johnson's decoration is surely a humdinger. She now wears smoked glasses to cover up the evidence. Some of the fishermen didn't fish for a week afterward.

No, I do not know the missing John Trager of Ben Hur Lodge.

No, we don't shoot fish. We sinfully gaff them. Then bing them with a big club. Then we cut their throat and rip their guts out. Then we boil them and eat them! What more can we do?

Outa Luck. Yesterday my snus box dumped over in the boat and all the precious stuff spilled out! Just one dam thing after another! Thunder, Lightning, Pouring Rain, Fog all day yesterday, last night and today. Man o Man! Will it ever let up ?—July 20, 1932

Doggone these pesky flies. They bit through my rubber boots. They surely can make a fellow say something not fit to be seen in print and we swear by them.

It happens here every day!

And doubtless the coroner's jury would call throat-cutting an "unavoidable accident" if it happened often.

We do it on purpose up here. And we don't give a dam for big or small throats either.

151

The Fish Scale

THE HERRING HAS NOTHING ON THE TROUT

Vol. 1   SEGLEM'S HARBOR, JULY 29, 1932.   No. 3

MEMBERS OF THE 500-CLUB DISCUSSING CURRENT TOPICS
(PUZZLE—FIND MA)

Go the Limit!

We are indeed glad to note in the last messages from home that Ma is able to go klatching in the extremely hot weather. It surely must take a lot of energy and melting resistance to endure it. But then on the other hand, see what a lot of fun she has. Man o man, what a real good time it must be to go places like that!

So we say—Go the Limit, Ma—and be glad you haven't got the Old Pest around to make it hotter for you. We sincerely hope you will be able to keep the ball arolling, but be careful how you step with that bum foot of yours lest it gets out of whack again. But—Go the Limit!

Thanks Terribly!

The last number (4) of the Hoozis to hand and contents noted. It is very interesting and we hope the hot weather you are so blessed with won't melt the editorial staff (stiff?) so soft or make them so weakly that they will be unable to keep up the good work. We are happy to say that we are not bothered with insomnia on account of heat. We simply dig ourselves down under a heavy blanket, a heavy quilt, and an Indian blanket on top of it all, then snore continuously till the birds sing the next morning. We sympathize with you, it must be terrible up in Mabel's room. We thank you all—Ye Ed, Ye CoEd, and Ye Able Assistant dear ma for all the news—good, bad and otherwise and the great amount of humor injected. Thanks terribly.

Scale Editor

LADIES AND GENTS! Here you see Ye Ed of the "Fish Scale" ardently at work getting out the next edition of the old bladder. The Editorial(?) sanctum is all in the picture but the dog's tail was accidentally cut off by the carelessness of Ye Ed. We are very comfortable—The weather is cool and bracing; the flapjacks are in the making; the java is brewing; the birds are singing; the fish is biting (lykell, lykell); the wind is howling (yessir); the lake is rough; the flies are eating us alive; the rain is pelting the roof and drips down on us in bed; the gulls are crying for more fish guts; the loony loon gives us the ha ha every time we lose a fish and the green grass is growing all around,*

But are we happy? By Krast*—we are so happy that we could yomp in the lake! and yomp twice at that. Today the sun shines warmly down on us and that adds to our pleasure, while at night we have beautiful moonshine (?) so you see, ladies and menfolks, we get along pretty good considering we are, so to speak, 3-in-One (No—not in one bed, but at the table).

And we are an ambitious bunch. Here are some of our daily doings: sawing and chopping wood, carrying water, washing clothes, washing dishes, baking bread, flipping flapjacks, picking berries, trolling, swearing at the wood stove, swatting flies, writing letters, bailing out the boats after the rains, etc. etc. etc.

CARETAKER AT ISLE ROYALE IS SUICIDE

After failing in what apparently was one suicide attempt, Joseph Engle, 45-year-old caretaker at a resort on Isle Royale, shot and killed himself there, Capt. Martin Christiansen of the fishing steamer Winyah reported on his return to Duluth. The body was found in a barn near the resort Wednesday with a 30.30 rifle lying beside it.

About ten days ago, Capt. Christiansen reported, he found Engle suffering from the effects of inhaling fumes from a gasoline engine. He brought him to Duluth for hospital treatment and on his recovery, returned him to the resort. Engle was single and had been caretaker at the resort for several years.

The body was taken to Calumet, Mich., by a coast guard cutter.

Sunday the kids beat me fishing. I caught one whopper weighing 3 1/2 lbs. and, by snakes, they went out and caught two! one a 2 Lbs. and one a 1 3/4 Lbs. I shamefully admit my defeat.

Adjust Complaint

For the Luv "O" Mike Roy, Wake up and please

"Don't-Snore"

like that," cries the young wife. "It gets a fella's nanny to be listening to that horrid noise! Saw your wood outside!"

"IS MY FACE RED?"

asks poor Eleanora. Answer: "See yourself as others see you, dearie." Or, "Yes, kid, as Red as a raw sirloin steak—and your poor, poor cornbeef nose has a piano polish hue with fish scales ornamentations on the tip of it. What more can you wish?"

Who told Hoss we had caught a 200-pound trout? He is all het up about it and telling everybody.

Up-to-date Invention

Roy surely is of an inventive mind. He has constructed an up-to-date fly or insect trap or contraption which has the old sparrow trap beat to a frazzle. In it he catches not only the pesky fly, but various other animules such as spiders, bumble bees, bugs, wasps, blowflies, yellow jackets, moths, microbes and angle worms. Oh, it's peacherino and he is thinking of having it patented. Too bad we have no bed bugs or it would be "lousy" with them. If he could only invent something to catch fish with we'd sit pritty.

Roy to Dad: "Do you think I can make er happy?"
Dad (confidently) to Sonny: "Well, she'll always have something to laugh at."

That's the Berries!

Dear Folks: You have nothing on us. We have a big dish of strawberries each to gladden our weary (?) hearts at our supper meals. Are they good? Nuh, they are simply delicatessen. Won't you come up and join us?

Sorry

indeed, to hear that the poor dear Ye Ed of our contemporary weak in the end Hoozis has such a hard (soft) time keeping from turning into soap grease. If he was up here the big fat Hot Tamale might turn into an icicle—so take your choice, Ye Ed. And we are Sorry also to hear that Ye Co-Ed has to be fed up on Eskimo Pie to keep from melting.

Pot Likker!

That surely was hot stuff we heard about Mustang, Red and Snuspick drinking Home Brew from the children's p pot. Man on man! That must have had a beautiful flavor. And we'll bet a trout skull that Mustang's face beamed like the intoxicating moon, and Red gleefully smacked his lips while old Snuspick drowned the delicious flavor with a "MorningMorning" washdown.

That kaffiyeek* "Stick" was more tame, but nevertheless, we can imagine the incident caused a big furor among the bunch.

3-in-One

Yes, dear folks, we're 3-in-one (no, not what you are thinking of—3-in-one bed—far be it from this.) We are three in one boat when we go fishing and always tow the other boat after us until we get to the reefs. There we separate—I take one boat, Roy and El the other.

The Newlyweds' Midsommer Night's Dream

That pillow, those mad nights of old,
Has seen our slumbering brows unite,
And 'neath the gondola's black fold
Has counted kisses infinite.

"Don't shoot the fish," you told us in the last Hoozis. We don't. We're no Chicago "holdup men up here. The only thing we do here is to swat the fly—and that's bad enough.

Duluth Retail Market Price:

Absolutely Fresh Caught
Trout, lb. 10c

Joys and Glooms
TAKE YOUR CHOICE

We haven't had a decent day for trolling since we came here.

The wind is taking the wind out of our joy sails day after day.

Got a dandy shyster lawyer from Rude the other day; it had a big fine liver and I made a fine meal out of it. But I had a heck of a time pulling the coat off the boy.

Eleanora sure knows how to fix up some swell eats, and she bakes like a veteran.

Today (Monday 25th) 5 a.m., a pouring rain storm set in accompanied by thunder and vivid flashes of lightning set in and its keeping on all day. And a gale blowing from Souwest.

Eric sent us a box containing salt pork, beans, bacon, Lux, and many other goodies. Guess he appreciates his stay.

Mrs. Rude brought us some delicious fruit soup and fish cakes the other day, and it sure was a treat.

Oh, Min! Soup's on. So is the Fish Scale.

Why Wifie Stayed Home.—"Aren't you taking your wife with you to the seaside?" "I'd like to, but you know yourself that the railroads refuse to take overweight baggage."—*Le Regiment.*

"And It Rained Cats and Dogs!"

Yessree! "It rained 'cats and dogs' last night, but we didn't mind it a bit. So we say too.

S·O·S

Send me a few one-cent stamps so I can punch George in the face every time I write home.

Hooper-Doo?

Say Co-Ed, wadda yuh mean by saying that The Fish Scale is a "Hooper-Doo?" The Scale cannot and will not tolerate such awful remarks. If it had come from other persons we sure would retaliate by bringing suit for slander or something. So be very careful, sweet Co-Ed, of what you say of The Fish Scale. If yah had said "Koga Doo*" instead of Hooper-Doo it wouldn't have been so bad.

Champion Fly Swatter

Roy has been decreed the champ fly swatter of Isle Royale National Park. He is constantly seen with the cruel swatter in his right hand scouting for the thirsty rambunctious blood suckers.

Here's a good idea. Try it next time you go to Indiana, Clarence, it will save a whole lot of swearing and Ma will be happy.

Is it hot nuff for U?

Discomfort in Chicago was relieved temporarily by a thunderstorm that struck the city after the temperature had risen to 97 degrees, a new record for the date.

Death came with the respite when lightning struck and killed a sandlot baseball player. Twenty others were stunned and shocked by the bolt.

The death toll in Chicago reached nine for the day with a three-day total of fifteen. Nearly all of these were deaths from prostration.

Up here we have fire in the stove to take the chill off; then we put on: union suit, pants, overalls, sweater, heavy wool shirt, another heavy sweater, then when it gets fresh we put a big raincoat on top of it all.

155

The Fish Scale

STEP ON IT EASY — DON'T JUMP ON IT

VOL. 1   SEGLEM'S HARBOR, AUGUST 3, 1932.   No. 4

MAMMA'S LITTLE DARLING GOING TO THE STORE

"Spring Moe En Fart!"

The Fish Scale has been politely informed by authentic authority that Mamma's little darling is now the official errand boy at 4514. We are pleased that he has been so appointed and we are confident that the dear little urchin will perform his dailies in a most efficient manner. This appointment is a great relief to the Scale Ed. as he knows that dear Mamma won't be pestered with his (YE ED'S) "pestiferations" for some-time to come. So run along, little boy, run along, and "Spring Moe En Fart!"*

July a Tuff Month

The month of July up here was certainly the limit for bum weather with Storms, Thunder, Lightning, Rain, Fog, and what have you, and in between this variety we had very little trolling weather, and aside from all this we had the Wind constantly blowing. But, neverthe-less, we caught 300 pounds of fish on our little spoon hook. The month of August is starting in with bet-ter weather and we have hopes of getting better results, if the weather behaves itself and the fish comes in on the reefs—but that is the main ?

Fishygrams

While I was out to the reefs and at Houghton Point trolling yesterday (Aug. 1), Roy and El stole out to the Rock reefs to try their luck and suddenly the sea got rough and they made for Boat Harbor a mile west of there. Luckily they had the "Almida" and the Elto in the boat. They tied up there and started to walk home, but changed their mind and set out again in the high sea for Seg's Harbor. We were getting anxious as to their absence and Mr. Rude and I set out in Rude's big fishing boat to try and locate the "Kids." Meantime the sea was getting rougher and the swells getting bigger. When we got clear of the breaking reefs and down along the coast about a mile, we met them coming bumping and hopping along with the Elto at 1/2 speed serenely smiling and evidently enjoying the rough ride. We offered to take them in tow but they gallantly refused our assistance, so we heaved to and followed them closely all the way to Seg's Harbor. It's mity lucky they had my boat and the motor or they probably would have had a hard pull on the oars before they reached Boat Harbor. All they got for their strenuous efforts was a little 2 1/2 pounder. I was lucky enough to catch 6 fish—25 pounds in all. So that's pretty fair for a start for August 1st. If luck is with us we may not have to walk back home.

Thanks Strekkeligt *

To Esther for that swell candy she sent. Oh it was surely good.

To dear Ma for telling us all about her strenuous Klatching. Go to it!

To Clarence for those much needed supplies for the motor. OK.

To Nurse Anna for that delicious cake. But we haven't received it yet (August 3d).

To the Ye Ed, Ye Co-Ed, and Ye Assistant Co-Ed for all the very interesting matter in the last No. of The Hoozis. Hope you won't get tired of sending us the "bladder."

Thanks to Manda for her dear letter. Glad to hear from her and Lillie. Please greet them from the Scale. To Vera for her HB; to Jennie for "Eat 'em while they're hot"; to Otto for that fancy fishbait he gave us.

Say, Dad, why can't I catch a big fish like you do? I'm sure I do my best to come up to you.

SEARCH ME, SONNY.

157

Eleanore says: "I am sure the one I lost was that big. Darn the luck!"

Roy-El's Big Haul

Last Sunday afternoon (July 31) Roy and Eleanora made a nice catch of Trout. They were out just a few hours late in the p.m. and caught eight nice fish. three 8 1/2 lbs., one 7 lbs; one 5 1/2 lbs; one 3 1/2 lbs; one 2 1/2 lbs; and one 1 pounder. This is one of their biggest hauls and they should be congratulated. They surely try mighty hard to do their part of the work and are on the lake whenever the weather permits. Eleanora enjoys being on the lake and she is a good rower and cheerful companion.

Here you see, folks, his majesty sitting serenely— perched on our fishhouse roof awaiting his doom. Alas! Then comes the cruel fisherman with his shooting iron and, bingo! It hits the mark and his majesty takes a flop. His broad wings and his mighty talons will be some day ornamenting the back porch at 4514.

Please Notice:

If you want mail or other things to reach us on Sunday's boat you must mail it not later than the Thursday preceding, and for the Wednesday's boat mail it not later than Saturday or Sunday preceeding. Otherwise it is liable not to reach us from 3 to 4 days later. Please bear this in mind.

A Snippy Answer

The other day I was flopjack hungry and I asked Roy to ask Eleanora to flip a bunch of the delicious shinplasters for lunch. And the gink grunted out in a somewhat doubtful tone:

ALASKA

Aigs - Again?

Roy says he hopes he don't have to peddle hen fruit again after he lands home. He'd rather peddle fish than eggs. But we surmise that Roy Watkins' hens will be laying for him again as usual.

Oh Vera! What's Happnd?

The hollow-eyed, the chaste Elvira came, Trembling and veiled, to view her traitor spouse, Was it one last bright smile she thought to claim, Such as made sweet the morning of his vows?

The sweet cartoon on the 1st page of No. 5 Hoozis picturing the Newlyweds on the swing was very appropriate for the occasion and we sincerely hope that when El has pulled out all of Roy's hair and he becomes bald headed that she still will love him as much as she does today.

Tell her: Don't take it off

In a "special dispatch" from our dearly beloved cousin Amanda she says: * * * "The only missing thing was our bathing suits, and believe me, I got one for the next trip, and it's coming off real soon." Oh, mamma! What a show it will be when IT COMES OFF. We hope "Aunty" Manda won't hang the bathing suit on a hickory limb while she takes a dip. A mosquito might have the nerve to land on her "wool soap"—and what a time the dear lady would have extracting the stinging apparatus. * * * *

Among other cheerful things she says: "A. L. Watts is on and off again." Well, we always thought he was a sort of a Banty Rooster, the old baldheaded rascal!

An Eye for an Eye

Funny things will happen. The other day Roy and Eleanora hookedup a fish and when Roy pulled in the line he found the fish's eye only on the hook. Now the poor fish is swimming around the lake winking his other eye and wondering what his other eye happened—and so is Roy.

Yes, Dear Co-Ed, It's Real

No, it's not a flake from Eleanora's "Corn Beef" Nose, nor the reflection from Roy's red beak, nor a piece of leather from Dad's weather-beaten neck—No, my dear, it's the genuine article—a real fish scale as you see, but it's all right in it's way, but it don't weigh much. Don't pick it off.

Bughouse Fables

Number 1

REMEMBER TH' BIG ONES WE CAUGHT UP IN TH' NORTH WOODS?

DON'T FORGET OLD TIGERTOOTH, TH' TWELVE-FOOT MUSKY, WHICH HOWIE CAUGHT!

Number 2.

Salary Increases 200% to 400%

3-in-1

Eleanora has "tresmag"—
Roy has "woolsoap" smag—
Dad has "Blaude Rou"—

Read it and Weep!

If you have cheers or tears for immediately foaming beers—to say nothing of a bottle a day to keep the bootlegger away—prepare to shed them now.

Row and Be

The wind is blowing on the lake
  Keep arowing!
The waves are following in its wake
  Keep arowing!
It's no use crooning, no use to yell,
The fish is biting—lykell, lykell,
And my SEAT is wet as a cup of jell,
  Keep arowing!   —Dad

"Fresh Fish! 8cts. a pound!"

Latest Weather Report:

A fearful road on a pitch dark night,
Lonely traveler.
For the wind and the rain they growl and bite—
Rain—rain on the roof.

159

Items of Interest?

The grass or hay around our cabins is taller than our head. *an our head.*

Flowers, flowers, wherever you go or see. Masses of the beautiful blomster all around us! *around us!*

Raspberries are now ripe and we pick them for jam which El puts up. Delicious indeed. *Delicious indeed.*

Blueberries are beginning to get ripe and we will soon go after them. *go after them.*

We have fresh lettuce and radishes from our garden every day. *day.*

We will soon have carrots too; they are growing fast. *ing fast*

We've had strawberries right along but now they are all gone. They were swell while they lasted. *lasted.*

The beautiful Gillardias are now in full bloom. A grand sight. *d sight.*

A couple (pair) of beautiful song birds are nesting about 3 feet from my window. I hope they won't abandon their nest when they get it built like the robin did. *robin did.*

The water in Lake Superior is this summer the highest it has been for 30 years and is steadily raising. *sing.*

We haven't heard or seen anything from the outside world since we got those newspapers from home about 6 weeks ago. We are getting very ignorant, indeed. *rorant, indeed.*

I have several bouquets of most beautiful flowers constantly on my table, and they surely help chasing the glooms away. *ooms away.*

The most comfortable items in my cabin is my snug bunk, my arm chair and my old rusty stove that makes the shack so cozy and warm when the storm rages on the outside. *outside.*

For what care I for wind or weather so let it roar *roar*
I lay my head upon the feather *for*
and simply snore. *snore.*
—Dad.

Har Du Lyst? Ya Visst! *

Whenever you see Roy, either in the boat or out, he always has *ys has*

The Pipe

in his face, and he looks very classic with the chimney puffing away like a rum runner after a bootlegger, while his pretty young wife stands by gazing admiringly. (?)

Well, I have to go and bail the rain water out of "Almida" again. She is half full of it after today's downpour.

The fog is obscuring the hillside across the bay, and the lake is in an ugly uproar. The reefs are breaking furiously, while the NorEaster is howling with madness.

Oh! It's a merry life sitting here in my snug cabin chasing flies and glooms.

But, we shall see the sun again and feel its life-giving warmth—Yes! We shall yet be happy!

Notes & Comments

We are glad to read about Ma Seglem's strenuous "Society" steppings and hope she may be able to carry on for a long time to come. Go to it, Ma.

Our boat "ALMIDA" can surely outride a stormy sea and skips like a duck from wave to wave. She had a very good tryout a few days ago and seems to stand it better than Rude's big fishboat.

See by the Hoozis that Art Tolzien has been on a big rampage lately. I'll bet there was some commotion when the storm broke loose. Gee! I'd like to have seen the fun.

Eleanora had a dream the other night that she caught a wonderful big fish. She says it was the funniest fish she ever saw. She had a hold of it, but it finally got away from her. It was a great disappointment to have such a dream and wake up in the morning and find there was nothing in it. Wasn't that terrible?

Say Ma, wouldn't this swell outfit be stunning in your society steppings? Oh, man. It surely would be an awful sensation along Jewish Boulevard, don't you think? I wish I could catch enough fish to pay for a rig like that. I hope that some day I will be able to buy you an outfit like this. Yes, I hope so, really.

Tell Vera not to forget to have a cold one all ready for us when we get home. Oh, boy, Oh boy, Oh boy! That sure will hit the spot. Wish I had one now.

Say Esther I wish you had been with me this morning (Aug. 3) down at the Point. I hooked up a 12 lbs. Then the wind blew up and I had to hike for home before it got worse. Well, the Winyah will soon be here so I have to cut it short for this time. —Dad

WADDA YOU SAY?

SEND me a few STAMPS so I can Scale - and also George. Send the Regularly pinch in the face. NE CENT STAMPS

161

The Fish Scale

THE SCALE WEIGHS A LOT, BUT IT TAKES A LOT OF SCALES TO TIP IT

VOL. 1　　　　SEGLEM'S HARBOR, AUGUST 10, 1932.　　　　No. 5

HAPPY, WHILE THE CAR IS PARKED HERE IN SOUTH BEND INDIANA, WE'LL GO OUT AND TRY TO CATCH SOME FISH.

ALL RIGHT, UNCLE JAKE. MAYBE WE CAN GET SOME POICH OR BLACK BASS.

I'LL TEAR OFF A NAP WHILE YOU'RE GONE.

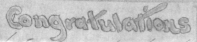

The Guy in the Center is the Wisest One in the Bunch- We Shay Sho!

Congratulations

The Scale hereby extends its hearty and sincere congratulations and greetings to the Co-Ed. of the Weakly Hoozis, dear little Esther, and wishes her many happy returns of the day. The only regrets we have is that we can't be with you on the happy occasion of your birthday to give you a genuine bear hug and slobber a fishy smack all over your face to show you how we love you.

Too Busy—Maybe?

We regretfully notice in the last Hoozis that the "Society" column has been omitted. What's the matter, Ma? Are you so busy stepklatching that you couldn't find time to say "Hello?" Or are you overcome with heat, swatting flies, or what? We sure hope the chief Ed didn't fire you.

Hello, Co-Ed, sorry to see that you too are so busy making pyjamas and step-ins that you couldn't find time to tell how hot it is.

BROADCASTING SWEET NEWS

Oh, Man; Oh, Man! Did we get a treat with last Sunday's Steamer—and it just came at dinner time. Here is what we received— No. 6 of The Hoozis bringing us all the latest news from Home and elsewhere. A copy of the Chicago Tribune putting us in contact with the Outside World at large—and here comes the best part of it, and it certainly cheered up three forlorn outcasts to the bottom of their hearts—That lovely delicious cake the Nurse baked—bless her kind heart— and according to the time you said it was mailed, it had been a week and a half in transit, but it came in good shape and it was just as fresh and toothsome as if it had been baked yesterday. Then too we received from E.T.'s folks a package containing 2 lbs. of coffee, a big bag of fresh plums, a big bag of peaches and some dandy solid tomatoes. The steamer came here about 12 o'clock noon and so the goodies arrived just in time for dinner. Yes, a thousand tak* to everybody who had a hand in thus cheering us up so surprisingly. It certainly was like a gift from heaven to be thus remembered in this lonely wilderness. Now we feel like a million dollars and don't give a heck whether it rains or shines

And here comes Mrs. Rude with a plateful of fishcakes for us! "It never rains but it pours" good stuff to eat upon us. These cakes were made from Menominee fish and were delicious to say the least. And are we thankful for all these good things? I'll say we are.

Our supply of potatoes is now Exhausted, so from now on we will have to fall back on the old conventional flap jack.

Good thing Brother Jiggs is not here. Our supply of corn beef is also exhausted. But shucks, who cares for cornbeef when we we have no cabbage

Our butter is now so "strong" that it walks from the fish house to the cabin, and Oh, what a flavor!

A pesky Owl makes a practice of landing on the roof of my cabin almost every night and has a merry old time scratching and screeching. Maybe she smells the old fish hawk within.

It is some bird family I have alongside of my window. I can look right into their pretty little nest. And how loving they are! Just like Roy and Eleanora. While the mamma bird is bringing forth her four baby birdlets papa bird brings her good things to eat such as bugs, flies, etc., and he takes his turn in sitting on the eggs. They sure set a beautiful example of domestic fidelity to us poor humans.

Thanks to my lucky stars, I still have some of my lovely "Baseman" left. And every once in a while I take a nibble from it. May it last forever!

163

Daily Doings

We have been having strawberries to our lunches for some time past.

Now we have delicious raspberry jam and pie from berries around here which are plentiful and ripe.

And the blueberries are also getting ripe. We are picking them every day.

Thimble berries will soon be ripe also. Then we will have some variety.

Roy keeps fit occasionally by snagging suckers at the dock.

Yessir! We are kept busy sawing and chopping wood, carrying water, washing dirty socks, washing dishes, and other funny things.

Roy has made a flytrap which is catching flies by the thousands.

Eleanora bakes 5 or 6 loaves of bread a week besides pies and making jam and biscuits. Some cook, she is!

In order to call me for the meals Roy rings a big cow bell which can be heard a half a mile away.

Well, I'll have to go and bail the rain water out of the boat—it's half full of it.

And Rain Ev'ry Day!

That an awakening wind bends over wrecking
seas,
Lost, flot a sail, a sail, a flowering isle, ere long?
But, O my heart, hear thou, hear thou, the sailors'
song!

Front seats not available. We therefor respectfully advise you to "Go 'way back and sit down." And do it without any back chinnin', too!

Maybe Otto Has the Malady!

"ACNE ROSACEA USUALLY STARTS WITH REDNESS AT THE END OF THE NOSE."

Glad to Hear It

We are indeed glad to note in your Hoozis that the home folks like The Fish Scale. The same can be said of The Hoozis. The old adage tells us that "A little nonsense now and then is relished by the best of men," and that goes for to pull down The Scale. There will probably not be very many more Scales issued, because we don't intend to stay here any later than Thanksgiving for we surely don't want to miss that Indiana bird.

Why So Crabby, Vera?

We'll drink only one glass at a time!

Here, girls and men-folks, you behold a a fair sight or view of the Scale's Editor's table decorations. We have constantly a big swell boquet of beautiful wildflowers before us to inspire us with cheerfulness from day to day.

My Little Bird Friend

My Little Bird Friend has built herself a cozy nest right outside of my window in a little bush and is now sitting on 4 pretty speckled eggs. She's so tame I can almost touch her with my hand. Her color is an olive green with a stripe of black around her head and she has a top knot.

We're trying to catch fish by telling them the jokes from The Weakly Hoozis, but they won't bite.

The Contest

The much advertised fishing contest between Roy and Dad is neck and neck to date. here is the score:

Roy Caught 78 fish —Total Wt. Round 304 lbs
Dad "   73 " " " "   514 "
    151 "   Total Wt "   818 "
Consumed for food about for our   100 "
                 718 "
Waste or cleanings — — — — 189 "
Total Shipped in Weight.   529 "

Roy is ahead in fish caught and Dad is ahead as far as weight goes.

The contest has been declared off as the trolling season is about done for this season. WHO WINS?

The Æroplane from Houghton, across the lake, passes Fisherman's Home occasionally.

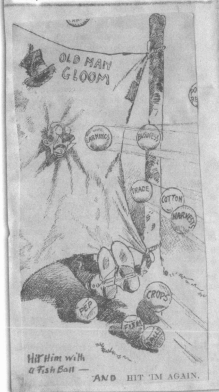

OLD MAN GLOOM

EARNINGS   BUSINESS   TRADE   COTTON   HARVEST   CROPS   PEP

Hit Him with a Fish Ball —
AND HIT 'IM AGAIN.

Weather Wheezes

We haven't had a perfect day since Eric was here. He was here in just the only time it's been nice.

We have had rain every day for the last two weeks.

While it may be nice on shore it is generally so windy and ruff on the lake that it is unhealthy to venture out.

Yesterday morning was nice and calm and we took a run out to McCormick's reefs, but as soon as we got there a stiff S.W. gale blew up and we had to hike for home without putting our hooks in the water.

Wouldn't it mar you, wouldn't it jar you—
       Wouldn't it make you sad?
He went out in the wind, stuck out his chin,
And the wind blew the moustache from Dad!

Just had a letter from Chas. Seglem. He says he can't come to Isle Royale this summer. His salary has been cut and his clerk laid off for 3 months. So he has to do all the work in his office all himself.

I sent E.T. a 7 lb. trout the other day with the Winyah and he says that both his and Tranvik's family had big meals from it. He surely appreciated the favor.

Bad Fire at Washington Harbor *

Mrs. Sam Sivertsen of Washington Harbor accidentally set fire to their net and warehouse and all their nets and everything they had in them were consumed by the blaze—the house burned to the ground. This was a big loss to the poor fisherman and it put him on the "rocks."

Famous Last Words:

GO TO

A&P

165

The Fish Scale

IT WILL NOT WEIGH ANY MORE FISH THIS SEASON

Vol. 1   SEGLEM'S HARBOR. AUGUST 17, 1932   No. 6

'ATTA-BOY, ALGERNON!'

DON'T   'SNUFF!

send any more papers or letters to us up here as we are planning on leaving as soon as we can arrange things, and if you don't hear from us for some time you may expect we are on our way. We have made no schedule of our return trip and therefore cannot tell when we will roll into the alley. Hope everything goes well on our home journey and that Roy's car will not lay down for us. It worked fine on the way up, and hope it will do likewise on the return trip. This issue of the Scale will probably be the last one as the Editor has gone on a strike for more $ and busted up the shop!

Yes, dear folks, 's nuff for this time. We've had our swing up here now for nearly 3 months—and, believe me, we've been "swinging" some too. We've used up nearly 40 gallons of gas which means that we've traveled 500 miles or more in the "ALMIDA" since we came here, if the distances were pieced together in one stretch. That's going some, I think. We have yet a distance of 80 miles to travel in our boat before we get to Grand Marais. We figure, if the weather is in our favor, that the trip will take 2 or 3 days, so that will complete our navigation. We now have good weather, but the fish seems to have gone into deep water and disappeared from the reefs. Very little is caught in the nets, too.

Otto and the Woodpecker

There was a great ball contest—no, not a ball game—football, basketball, handball or fishball, but a game of pitching, sort of a target pitching contest something like knocking the babies down at Riverview. It was held in a big hall aud and we stood in the doorway watching the sport. There were Emil, Clarence, Otto, John, and a number of others taking part in the pitching game to see who could hit the target across the Hall. Oh ho! Clarence's first shot. He came within a few inches of hitting the mark. Then came the turn to Mustang. Zowie! Didn't hit it, but pretty close. Then one by one had their turns, but none could come closer than the other. "Ah!" says Otto, "give me the ball." Well, he got it and taking deliberate aim he started to swing his arms like a windmill in a Holland hurricane, and zingo! the ball went sailing toward the target but, oh my! he missed it by about three feet. And did he get razzed! And as the gang all give Snuspick the ha ha, I woke up! It was but an Isle Royale dream.

x x x

Here's a good one, this time on me. This morning (Sunday) about 5:30 A.M. I heard a knocking, and thinking it was Roy waking me to go out trolling, I jumped out of bed as fast as the Lord would let me, shouting "All right, I'm up" and rushing to the door, again shouting: "Do you want to come in?" Well, I opened the door and found, to my surprise that there were nobody there. This I thought was queer as I surely heard the knocking or tapping just a few minutes before. Well, I went to investigate (in my shirttail) and found a galldarned woodpecker merrily sitting on the radio mast attached to the corner of my cabin tapping for all he was worth. And to my great chagrin I had asked the pesky bird if he wanted to come in! A "horse" on me!

Well, folks, if I had had a shotgun it would have been just too bad for Mr. Woodpecker, but as it was I picked up a rock and swinging my right arm like Otto, let it sail with all my might at that darned pesky peckerhead, but of course, I missed my mark and Mr. Pecker simply sat there and continued to tap tap tap.

Trolling at End

The trolling season is now past and no matter how we try or what lure we use we don't get a nibble any more. The best time for this sport is during June and July. But the weather during those months was steadily against us so we didn't get much of a chance to go after the "big" ones, but nevertheless we hooked up a few and have to be satisfied with what we got. We will soon kiss Isle Royale a sweet goodbye perhaps never to return, as conditions up here are not what they used to be in former years when fishing was at its best.

A Beautiful Trip

Last Saturday there was no fish to be caught on troll. After repeated trying, we decided to take a trip to Malone Island, 10 miles across the broad Siskiwit Bay, to visit our friends John Skadberg and Ed Ronning and Ben Benson. The weather was fine and the lake as smooth as glass with the sun beating its hot rays down upon us. In fact, an ideal day for an outing. We started out about 1 o'clock p.m. and motored with a weak battery but got there after about 1 1/2 hours run. Eleanora brought along a dandy 2-layer chokolate cake and a fresh loaf of bread which put joy in the hearts of the Malone fisherman's camp. Here we had a bumper lunch of fried ham, corn-beef, bread, butter, cake, and Coffee, and Roy got the motor in shape with one of John's storage batteries. About 6 p.m. we started on our return trip and called in at Sam Johnson's at Wright's Island, 2 miles west. There with the help of Ed Holte, Roy got the motor in good running order. They invited us in for supper and El and Mrs. Holte (Sam's daughter) got quite chummy. They are nice people from Grd. Marais. We staid there till 8 o'clock, then the moon came along and lit up the lake and in the boat we jumped and set off on a glassy moonlit sea for Seglem's Harbor across the wide Siskiwit Bay, 8 miles to the Souwest. It was the most beautiful boat trip I have ever had, a most enchanting journey with the pale full moon casting its silvery beams in a romantic, fascinating ecstasy on the calm sea which in turn cast a shaft of silver across our port side. We sang, we shouted, we laughed—and the newlyweds, especially El, was deeply entranced with the grandeur of that memorable moon light trip across the broad Siskiwit Bay. We made the trip in one hour and ten minutes.

Blueberries on I.R.

Something new to me. We dis-cover blueberries growing up the ridge and they are big and juicy. We are picking can after can and have them on the table every day as sauce, etc., and Eleanora is busy feeding us delicious juicy pie from those dainty pretty little morsels. There are also a lot of fine raspber-ries everywhere, right near our cabins which we also make good use of for pies, sauce and jams. And now the Indian plums are ripe and the thimbleberries are ripening fast also—all around us, so we are kept busy picking and eating of all those good things. Wish we could can in some and take home with us.

Yes, we have no—

(ACTUAL "LIFESIZE" BOY)

Thank the good Lord, we are no more pestered with these bloomin' blood suckers. The blackflies are also gone and the biting "houseflies" have also disap-peared. So life up here is not bad now at all. The only thing we now look for is good weather for our home sailing and if luck is with us we'll be jake.

Thanks

for the letter and papers Esther and for your snappy squibbs in the Hoozis. Also to Ma for her cheery "society" news, and a fish box full of thankyahs to the able YE ED for all the interesting reading matter.

Fish Guts

The wolves across our little bay are howling and yelling every night.

I dreamt last nite I jumped off from a high ledge onto big rocks far below, and as I landed let out a loud whoop "Oih!" which Mrs. Rude thought was from a coyute.

Thanks for those stamps I asked for and didn't get.

I was just now about 3 feet from my door and filled myself with nice juicy red raspberries. The bushes stand red with them everywhere. And they are GOOD.

An Æroplane just flew by our place.

Today we are having an exceptionally hot day. Thermometer 77°. (Tuesday)

Giddup, Napoleon! It looks like rain.

We had a big kick out of last week's "Hoozis." Especially Eleanora and her "tresmag."

Oh man! The Blueberry Pie is the Cat's pyjamas!

Chicago, Here We Come!

*Don't know, but we hope this will not be the way we have to travel on our homecoming, but you can't never sometimes tell all the vile. But a ride on the bumpers is better **than** hoofing it all the way **back** for 700 miles or more, **by heck!***

here, dear folks, you see our little friend "JOY" speeding us on with his gladdening signal "Go" which means so much to the weary wayfarer. May he greet us everywhere on our home journey.

MINUTE THAT SEEMS A YEAR.

FAMOUS LAST WORDS — "IT WON'T BE LONG NOW."

Notes

1920: Fisherman's Home Journal

June 14

Steamer: The America, which plied Lake Superior delivering mail, freight, supplies, and passengers from 1902 to 1928, when it ran aground and sank at the mouth of Washington Harbor on the western end of Isle Royale.
Alice: Elling and Almida Seglem's daughter.

June 15

G. M.: Elling often writes G.M. for A.M., probably a joke for good morning.
Edward: Edward T. Seglem or E.T., Elling's cousin.
Ma: Elling's wife, Almida.

June 16

Siskiwit Bay: Present spelling of the largest bay on Isle Royale, located along the southern shore of the island. Other spellings are Siskowit, Siscowit.
Redfin Island: An island in Siskiwit Bay, about a mile and a half ENE of Point Houghton.

June 17

Magda: E.T. Seglem's daughter.
Mrs. Seglem: E.T.'s wife, Alida.
JERUSHA: This seems to be the name Elling uses when writing in his daughter Alice's voice.

June 18

Martin Halloran: Halloran was a fisherman whose cabin was located inland on Lake Halloran; to reach it he often poled a raft across the lake to the eastern end where his cabin was located.

June 19

Skoan Bred: biscuits or "dropped scones."

June 20

På samma gongen... Go-na-at.: (Norwegian) Translation: "At the same time, may I greet all those at home, from the basement to the roof. Good Night."
Wolves: Although some individual wolves may have managed to cross to Isle Royale, a breeding pack only established itself on the island after 1948; from the early 1900s to the 1950s the island had a population of

coyotes, or "brush wolves," until the wolves eliminated them. It is uncertain which Elling heard.

Hans: Hans Mindstrom, fisherman from Little Boat Harbor.

June 21

the girls: E.T.'s daughters.
Capt: Edward "Indian" Smith, Captain of America 1910-1928.

June 22

Maccabee initiation: Knights of the Maccabees were a fraternal and "benevolent" organization founded in 1878 and renamed simply the Maccabees in 1914. Like other organizations such as the Masons, the Shriners, and the Knights of Columbus, it had elaborate rituals and membership ranks. It was especially known for paying insurance benefits to the families of deceased members. In 1962 the social aspect of the organization was dissolved and the society became an insurance company, Maccabees Mutual Life.

Rocks: McCormick Rocks are shallows off the south shore of the island, about two and a half to three miles west of Fisherman's Home and the tip of Point Houghton. McCormick Reefs are another two and a half to three miles further west.

June 23

Almida: Elling's wife.
hell divers: Grebes, especially pied-billed grebes.

June 24

Kogefisk: The Norwegian term is kokefisk, meaning either boiled fish or enough fish for a meal.
Edith, Lala, Elleanore: E.T.'s children.

June 25

Esther: Elling's daughter.

June 26

lawyers: A "lawyer" is a burbot, a fish with distinctive "barbels" or "beards" above and below its mouth.

June 27

Little Siskiwit Bay: There is no Little Siskiwit Bay, unless Elling means the inlet of Hay Bay at the mouth of the Little Siskiwit River, or an inlet on Little Siskiwit Island about three miles due north of Point Houghton.

June 30
cave, skeletons: The cave had been the sealed burial site of Native Americans exposed and opened by the weather.
Barnum: George Barnum was a grain merchant in Duluth who bought an island near Washington Harbor.

July 1
Menominee: The menominee or round whitefish is also known as pilot fish, frost fish, and menominee whitefish.
Thora: E.T.'s niece.

July 2
Boat Harbor: Little Boat Harbor is located on Lake Superior a little more than two miles southwest of Point Houghton.

July 4
Clar: Elling's son, Clarence.
Otto, Vera: Relatives in Chicago. Otto Nelson is Almida's brother.
Jenny: Jenny Nelson, Elling's sister-in-law.
Roy: Elling's son.

July 6
Attwood beach: On the coast of Siskiwit Bay above Point Houghton.

July 10
Dalrymple: Elling is making a joke about Prohibition. Major A.V. Dalrymple was the supervising prohibition director for the Central Division and earlier in 1920 had led an armed force to seize bootleg wine in a community in the Upper Peninsula. The Iron River Rum Rebellion challenged the legality of prohibition tactics of search and seizure and Dalrymple's actions were widely publicized.

July 11
Abe Olsen: A relative in Iowa.
Russell Arch: A relative.
Mostar: An aunt.
Manda: Amanda, a cousin.

July 14

"Skrydt shelf, jug har inte ted": (Norwegian) Translation: "Do it yourself. I don't have time."

home in Norway: Elling was born in Seglem, Norway, and became a naturalized American citizen.

July 15

eelpouch, låke: The Swedish word "låke" refers to the eelpout or burbot.

Ma Knows: Almida Seglem was Swedish.

Capt. Purdie: Charlie Purdie, fisherman at Wright Island, married to Ingeborg Holte's sister Alice.

July 18

Viroqua: A small town in western Wisconsin, southeast of La Crosse, it was a successful dairy and tobacco farming community heavily populated with Norwegian immigrants.

Hooch: Liquor. A reference to Prohibition, which stayed in effect until 1933.

W.T. at Standard Rock: E.T.'s sister was married to someone with the initials W.T. Standard Rock is between Duluth and Grand Marais near Beaver Bay. He may be referring to Split Rock.

July 19

wolves: See note for June 20.

July 24

Kaffeslaberas: Norwegian for "coffee party" or "coffee klatsch."

July 25

Hotel: Elling's term for a bunkhouse at the Seglem fishing camp.

July 29

Hilda, Lillie: Cousins in Chicago.

July 31

Krixnix Kolumpus: Elling's Norwegian pronunciation of Christopher Columbus. The Christopher Columbus was a whaleback excursion steamer which operated between 1893 and 1932 and was scrapped in 1937. In 1920 it advertised in the Chicago Tribune that it offered "dancing, café, lunch rooms, and 4 broad shady decks" and cruised from Chicago to Milwaukee and back in twelve hours, "in sight of land all the way."

1921: Diary
May 22
firlings: Elling may simply mean "the children." In Swedish, a fyrling is a quadruplet.

May 23
John and Gertie: John and Gertie Seglem, E.T.'s nephew and niece, children of E.T.'s brother Johan.
E.T.'s house: E.T. and his family lived at 2618 West 5th Street, Duluth.
Mr. Melby: Relative of E.T. Seglem.

May 24
Thorvald: E.T. Seglem's son who later drowned in a boating accident near Duluth. (Correct spelling is Thorwald.)
John: Probably John Seglem, E.T.'s nephew.
Morgan Park: A model town built along the St. Louis River by the United States Steel Corporation for its employees.

May 25
steamer dock: The America dock.
Lester Park: On the lakeshore north of Duluth, Lester Park is 47 acres with pines, footpaths, and a trout stream.
Pete Skadberg: Brother of Isle Royale fisherman, John.

May 26
Thorvald from Standard Rock: Thorvald Midbrod.

May 27
Pike Lake: An inland lake, about twelve miles northwest of Duluth.

May 28
New Duluth, Gary: Both are about five miles southwest of Duluth, along the St. Louis River.

May 30
Fort William, Port Arthur: Sister cities located in Ontario now known as Thunder Bay.
Belle Isle, Tobin: In the 1920s two of the resorts on the eastern end of the island were Belle Isle Resort, located on the north shore on Belle Isle, and Tobin's Resort, located on Minong Island in Tobin Harbor.

Menagerie Light: Menagerie Island was one of the easternmost of a chain of reefs and islands extending out from Point Houghton at the entrance to Siskiwit Bay and was the location for Isle Royale Lighthouse, built in 1875.

June 1
Olaf: Seems to have been a hired man working for E.T. Seglem.

June 2
George: Probably another hired man.

June 3
Tette some potta: (Norwegian) Translation: "Watertight as a chamber pot."

June 8
Francis Reef: Maybe a shallows of Francis Point.

June 11
Kompa: Means "to accompany" in Norwegian, so Elling is probably saying that he had company for dinner.

June 22
Falk: A Chicago photographer.

June 23
Aleck, Edwin: Relatives.

June 26
Hay Bay: An arm of Siskiwit Bay, due north of Point Houghton.
Obert, Hansen, Bjorvek: Alex Oberg, Andrew and Mary Hansen, Albert Bjorvek, who fished from a location in Hay Bay.

July 10
Julius: A hired man.

July 21
Margretha: Margretha Anderson was E.T.'s sister, Elling's cousin.

Aug 4
"Stella": Sam Rude's boat.

1923: Diary
June 7
John, Mamie: Mamie and John Pedersen were cousins in Chicago.
North American: The train from Chicago to Duluth.

June 8
Tronvick: Thora Tronvick was E.T.'s sister and Elling's cousin.

June 9
Minnesota Point: One of the two narrow sandbars (the other is Wisconsin Point) at the mouth of Duluth Harbor.

June 28
"Norlands Jachter": (Norwegian) Translation: "Yachted for Norland."

July 1
Bjorvek and Kvalvick: Albert Bjorvek and Ed Kvalvick, fishermen from Hay Bay.

July 6
Skolt: Norwegian word for skull or top of head; may be Elling's play on fish head.

1924: Diary
June 3
Kalsomined: Calcimine is a white wash for walls and ceilings.
"traps": Trappings, belongings.

June 17
Visergutten: Visergutten was a Norwegian-American newspaper published in Story City, IA 1895-1918 and Canton, SD 1918-1944. In the June 18 entry Elling draws a hand pointing to the bottom of the opposite page and the words "Visergutten. Poem-E.A.S.," indicating that he sent the newspaper a poem.

June 20
Anderson & Olson: Fishermen from Tobin and Rock Harbor.

June 24
Wright's Island: In the northeast corner of Siskiwit Bay.

R.I.: Probably Ross Island, a large island east of Wright Island and further along the coast toward Rock Harbor.

June 25

Mike Johnson: Rock Harbor fisherman.
old Light house: The Rock Harbor Lighthouse, near the Middle Passage, was the first lighthouse on the island, built in 1855.
Cemetery Island: A small island near the Middle Passage into Rock Harbor, it has grave markers of miners from the first period of copper mining.

June 26

Mr. Rude: This was Andrew Rude. He worked for the Seglems as hired man in the early 1920s and then began fishing for himself at Fisherman's Home. His wife and his son, Sam, also fished with him.

July 10

Otto Gronbeck: A friend from Chicago.

July 12

Francis Point: This point is on Siskiwit Bay, three miles west of the tip of Point Houghton.

July 25

Johnson Island and Thompson Island: Both are near Washington Harbor. Johnson Island is now called Johns Island.

August 2

Sivertsen: Sam Sivertson was a fisherman in Washington Harbor.

1932 "A Record of the Isle Royale Trip"

June 2

Cary, Woodstock, Harvard: Locations in Illinois.
Walworth, Darien... Readstown, Viroqua: Locations in Wisconsin.
The Newlyweds: Elling's son Roy and his new wife Eleanora.

June 3

La Crosse: Last stop on western boundary of Wisconsin.
Winona... Duluth: Locations in Minnesota.
Tronvick and Seglems: Otto and Thora Tronvick, E.T. and Alida Seglem.

June 4

G. M.: Grand Marais. Elling and his son and daughter-in-law intend to drive to Grand Marais and meet the steamer there rather than take it from Duluth.

June 7

Winyah: The steamer America sank in 1928 and the Winyah took over the route between 1930 and 1943.

June 12

Eric: A relative, possibly a grandson.

June 13

Siskiwit River: Probably Big Siskiwit River, which empties into the western end of Siskiwit Bay below Senter Point.

June 16

Ronning: Ed Ronning, a fisherman.

June 30

rug Kavring: Norwegian for rye roll.

July 3

Santoriam Reefs: Elling undoubtedly means San Antonio Reef, near Harlem Reef, in a direct line with Paul Island and due east from Redfin Island. This may be a deliberate mispronunciation or simply a mistake.

July 4

Mr & Mrs. Sivert Anderson: Hay Bay fishing couple.
Johnson: Holger and Lucy Johnson and their five children lived at Chippewa Harbor; it was their family Dorothy Simonsen taught when she and her son Bob wintered over with them on the island in 1932-1933.
Smålending: Someone from Smaland, one of the poorest regions of Sweden, from which many people immigrated to the U.S.

July 5

Otto Olson: A cousin of Holger Johnson.

July 10

"Hoozis": "The Weakly Hoozis" was a mock newspaper, perhaps in imitation of Elling's "Fisherman's Home Journal" of 1920, put together by members of the family in Chicago to send to Isle Royale. Elling responded with "The Fish Scale," his mock newspaper of 1932, and Roy and Eleanora sent off one of their own, "The Fish News."

July 23
Ed Holte: A fisherman from Wright Island, the son-in-law of Sam Johnson.

July 30
Troll kjerringen: Norwegian for female troll or witch, an allusion to Norse folklore but also a joke on the woman's activity (trolling). The woman with whom he is making the comparison is unknown, perhaps Mrs. Rude.

Aug 6
Rude Spoon: A spoon is a shiny, curved, metallic fishing lure; Elling must have gotten this one from Andrew or Sam Rude.

Aug 7
Nursie Anna: Elling's daughter-in-law.

Aug 15
austgespielt: Norwegian for "played out."

Aug 20
Long Point: Near the southwest corner of Isle Royale, just where the island starts to curve toward the northwest.

Aug 21
Susie Island: Susie Island is one of several islands just below Pigeon Point and the U.S.-Canadian border, along the Minnesota shoreline.
Rocky Point: Elling may mean Red Rock, a point which forms Deronda Bay along the Minnesota coast eight to ten miles southwest of Susie Island.

Aug 22
"5-Mile Rock": A landmark northeast of Grand Marais.

Aug 23
Bev Bay: Beaver Bay, about 45 miles northeast of Duluth along the coast.
Palisade Blueberry hill: Palisades Head is a rocky formation a few miles north of Beaver Bay.

Aug 24
K. R.: Knife River
Christiansen: Martin Christianson, fish buyer on board the Winyah (H.Christianson and Sons Fish Co.).

1932: The Fish Scale
July 10
Sharkey and Schmelling: Boxers who fought for the World Title in 1930.
Park Place: The resort at Snug Harbor, where Rock Harbor Lodge is now; it was renamed Rock Harbor Lodge in 1922 but Elling calls it by its former name.
Tourist Home: Located on Davidson's Island east of Mott Island in Rock Harbor.

July 20
lykell: Elling's way of saying "like hell."
Zar Christianson: Perhaps a deliberate misspelling of Czar in reference to the fish buyer on the Winyah.
Kate Smith: A singer. Elling is probably using the tune of her signature song "When the Moon Comes Over the Mountain" for his song about Red and Snuspick.

July 27
green grass is growing all around: The chorus of a children's song by that title, suggesting that the list that precedes it is imitating the list in the song.
By Krast: Norwegian for "By Christ."
kaffi yeek: Perhaps "kaffegok" which is coffee laced with akvavit, which is similar to vodka.

Aug 3
"Spring Moe En Fart": Norwegian meaning "hurry up."
Skrekkeligt: Norwegian for "very much."
Har Dulyst? Ya Vist!: Norwegian for "Do you want to? Yes, of course!"

Aug 10
tak: Norwegian for "thanks."
Bad Fire at Washington Harbor: Elling did not know at the time that one of Sivertsen's fishing rivals quietly brought him replacement nets out of his own supply so that he could continue fishing.

Further Reading

Tim Cochrane and Hawk Tolson. *A Good Boat Speaks for Itself: Isle Royale Fishermen and Their Boats.*
Minneapolis: U. of Minnesota Press, 2002. An account of the people, wooden boats, and folkways of the Isle Royale fishing community.

Thomas and Kendra Gale. *Isle Royale: A Photographic History.*
Houghton: Isle Royale Natural History Association, 1995. The history of Isle Royale from early exploration to the birth of the national park as told through historical photographs and maps.

Dave Harmon, editor. *Borealis.*
Houghton: Isle Royale Natural History Association, 1992. A collection of stories of the people who helped shape the history and legends of Isle Royale.

Smitty Parratt and Doug Welker. *The Place Names of Isle Royale.*
Houghton: Isle Royale Natural History Association, 1999. A short Isle Royale history in itself, this book includes the origins, histories, and stories of over 250 Isle Royale locations.

Dorothy Simonsen. *Diary of an Isle Royale School Teacher.*
Houghton: Isle Royale Natural History Association, 1992. In this private journal Dorothy Simonsen tells of the joys and hardships of the winter of 1932 which she spent on Isle Royale as a school teacher to a fisherman's family.

Howard Sivertson. *Once Upon An Isle: The Story of Fishing Families on Isle Royale.*
Mount Horeb: Wisconsin Folk Museum, 1992. Paintings and stories of the everyday lives of the families that fished Isle Royale in the 1930s and 1940s.